MW00698080

DIVORCED AND FORTY

CONQUERING DIVORCE WITH YOUR SENSE OF HUMOR INTACT

CODY FIFE

Copyright 2019 Cody Wright

ALL RIGHTS RESERVED. This book contains material protected under International and Federal Copyright Laws and Treaties. Any unauthorized reprint or use of this material is prohibited. No part of this book may be reproduced or transmitted in any form or by any means, electronic or mechanical, including photocopying, recording, or by any information storage and retrieval system without express written permission from the author/publisher.

Paperback: 978-1-64184-111-5
ebook: 978-1-64184-112-2

Transformation

The browns and grays of winter show themselves
to be my friends.

They remind me that this too shall pass, like the seasons
have their end.

The barren branches of the trees outstretched like
open hands

Are waiting for the time to pass, for life to come again.

The bleak and barren fields are still.

There is no use to fret

Or sing a sad lament for time

Or what they can't forget.

They sit and wait

And know one day

They will again be clothed in green

For the darkest days of Winter

Must give way unto the Spring.

—Cody Fife

DEDICATION

To be alive is to be broken. And to be broken is to stand in need of grace.

Brennan Manning, *The Ragamuffin Gospel*

To Mom and Dad,

Thank you for feeding me bread pudding and not letting me die of starvation when I was so heartbroken I couldn't eat and was starting to resemble the bride of Skeletor. Also, thank you for keeping me from being homeless or having to live in a seedy apartment complex. In addition, thank you for picking up the parenting slack when I couldn't be in three places at one time or just completely forgot I was supposed to pick up a child and was still at work. Lastly, thanks for getting me that typewriter with the cool correcting tape circa 1987 and the "How to Type" book. That really did come in handy with this whole "I think I'll write a book" thing. But mostly, I would like to thank you for simply being there when I needed you the most. I love you.

To Kevin Baker,

Thank you for showing me it was possible to fall in love and trust again and for being so worthy and deserving of that trust. I am thankful that our paths crossed at just the right time.

TABLE OF CONTENTS

AUTHOR'S PREFACE

Blackbird singing in the dead of night, take these broken wings and learn to fly. All your life you were only waiting for this moment to arise.

John Lennon/Paul McCartney

I began writing this book after attending Tom Bird's "Write to Heal" writing workshop in Sedona, Arizona in June of 2017. I ended up in Sedona the way I ended up in many new places I never expected to be -- by the grace of God. I happened to attend a church service one Sunday at the Unity Church in Houston, Texas as a visitor, and in the church bulletin was an insert about a class Tom was holding at the church. While I couldn't attend that particular weekend retreat, I got online, researched him, and signed myself up for his summer, "Write to Heal" retreat. I did just that: I started writing, and I started healing. I was broken: completely and utterly broken. I was also determined: determined not to stay that way. I was in need of God's grace. I was in need of God's love, and God was so faithful to meet me right in the middle of my big, muddy mess of a life. This book was written along different moments of my journey through the shock and anger of betrayal and the grief of divorce. I was devastated and trying my best to wrap my brain around what had just happened. Writing helped me to do that. I threw away the first 30,000 words I wrote because they were so depressing and angry no one would have wanted to read them! I certainly didn't. They were simply cathartic, and I had to get them out of the way before I could write anything with a half-way clear mind. I tried to find some humor along the way and include it in this book. I cried more in the six months after my marriage fell apart than I knew was humanly possible. I knew that in the middle of my misery, I would find relief in comedy. Sometimes, things can be so ridiculous, you just have to laugh. Plus, I don't really hang out with people who don't have a sense of humor, so there was always someone I could call crying to and end up laughing with.

There were moments I wrote when I was in deep sadness, and there were moments I wrote when I had profound peace. There were also moments I was angry, really angry. I tried not to write when I was too angry, but it did help me to get it out onto the page. After a year of writing, I can say that the way I look at my divorce and the shock of how my marriage ended has been transformed. I have been transformed. It has been an incredible journey of spiritual and personal growth. I can look back at the last two years and see how God brought people, books, and events into my life in the most miraculous ways to guide me along my personal journey to healing. There are no coincidences, and if you connect to the infinite Source that is present everywhere, in all of us, there will never be an end to the learning, the growing, and the beauty that life has in store for us. So, if your life has been derailed by betrayal and divorce, I hope this book will give you hope, make you laugh, and help you know that the rollercoaster of emotions you are feeling are normal. I also hope it is a reminder that any negative feelings you are experiencing about yourself, your life, and your future in the divorce fallout are only temporary.

Please know that I am no expert. While I have a master's degree in counseling psychology, I knew nothing of the process of grief and the complex emotions and psychological rollercoaster of divorce until I experienced it first-hand. Also, please know that I am no spiritual expert or claim to be one in any way. I read a lot. I've always gone to my Bible when life's storms hit, but I am by no means the perfect Christian. You know that t-shirt that says, "I love Jesus, but I cuss a little?" Me. I listened to a lot of spiritual teachers ranging from the likes of Wayne Dyer, Louise Hay, Pam Grout, Alan Cohen, Marianne Williamson, John Gray, Joyce Meyer, and Charles Stanley in my pursuit to be whole again. I have tried my best to document my opinions and experience so that perhaps it will help even one other person on their own journey to know that they are not alone.

I am no expert. I am just a girl who fell in love, got her heart broken, and winged her way through trying to put the pieces back together again. So, here's to winging it. May we all learn to fly again.

FORGET THE GLASS SLIPPER

Well, here we are -- divorced and forty. I use the term "forty" lightly. It's more of an estimate. I'm actually forty-one. I know; it's just a number. So is the number two, as in, "How many times have you been divorced?" My answer: "Twice."

I hate that answer, "Twice." It's a little embarrassing, I admit. I'm trying to move from shame to acceptance, but maybe that's a little too much to ask of myself too soon. You see, this wasn't my plan. This wasn't my plan at all. I'm guessing it wasn't in your plans either, but here we are.

As a little girl, you imagine yourself "grown up" and married, with a handsome husband, 2.5 kids, a white picket fence, a sensible four door family sedan, and a quaint little Victorian home picturesquely situated on some "Sound of Music" green hill.

What you don't imagine is the worst-case scenario coming true. You don't imagine your husband turning into a complete jackass, your kids having to move out of their comfortable

1

family home and neighborhood, your pristine picket fence getting smashed to bits by a bulldozer, your sensible sedan tires slashed, and your green hill drying up into a crunchy, brown mound of dead grass.

You don't imagine yourself in the future scene that I had the horror of living in real life on the heels of my separation (We'll get to that story later.) discovery (Not the legal type, which you are likely familiar with if you are going through a divorce, but the find-the-card-from-the-other-woman type), the filing (He filed), the mediation (Send in the clowns), the waiting (Please God, just let it be over so I can get closure), the final hearing (I didn't go), and the signing of the final decree.

Exhale.

It felt like seven months of holding my breath ... with an elephant sitting on my chest.

Picture this. It is October, and it's a Friday. It's the first Friday of the month, so it's dad's weekend to get the kids. In my case, it's dads' weekend to get the kids. Two dads, three kids, and a lot of complicated logistical juggling ... welcome to my life. So, there I was, exhausted from a week of teaching seventh graders, trying to be a good mom to my own three, and crying pretty much every second of my waking hours in between those responsibilities. I was devastated. I was broken. I was confused. I was a hot mess. I felt defeated, but Friday had arrived, and I would at least get a little rest.

It was about 6:00 p.m. My first ex-husband arrived to pick up my two oldest kids, fifteen and twelve years old. He happened to show up that day with his newish wife in tow. At this point we've been divorced so long it's not weird anymore, but I felt embarrassed and ashamed that they obviously knew I was getting divorced again. They normally just drive up, the kids jump in the car, and they drive away. Simple, right? Well, it wasn't simple on this particular fall day.

I look out of my window and see my ex, the first one, talking to my dad in the driveway. You see, I moved back home, right next door to my parents in my grandparents' old house. They are discussing when he can come to teach our son how to hunt on the ranch. They discussed and discussed for what seemed like for freaking ever.

It had been about twenty minutes of discussion, and they were all standing in my driveway: the first ex, his wife, their toddler, and my two kids. I knew my "husband" was on the way that very moment to get my youngest daughter, my five-year-old, and I started to panic. Just seeing my "husband" for the few moments it took to exchange our daughter was excruciatingly painful. Every single time I had to see him, I was upset for hours afterward. I was angry, hurt, and humiliated. It had only been a month since I figured out he was already in a relationship with another woman while I had been praying and holding onto hope for reconciliation. Talk about feeling like a fool. I certainly did.

It was bad enough just seeing him. The thought of having to face him and my ex-husband and his new wife plus my shame and heartache all in one place, the one place that had become my hiding place and sanctuary, my home, felt overwhelmingly awful. I imagined the announcer's voice from the old school Price is Right, you know the one with

Bob and not Drew, playing like a sound track over the whole catastrophic scene. "Cody Fife, come on down! You're the next lucky contestant on 'Your Life Ain't Right!' Come on down your driveway, and let's take a look at today's showcase. Oh, look! It's your life failures!"

I walked next door and stood in the kitchen with my mom, anticipating the impending scene of a convention of exes taking place at the foot of my sidewalk. I appealed to my mom like I was a fourteen-year-old begging to be taken to meet her friends at the movie theater in town.

"Mom. Seriously, can you please go distract dad and give him the old elbow nudge that it's time to wrap it up? I mean, what are they even still talking about? Can't they just leave?"

She was at a loss. Then, what do you know? Before I could continue begging her to feign some kitchen emergency requiring my dad's immediate intervention and hasty exit from the scene of impending humiliation, I hear the rumbling of a truck approaching. There came the "husband" in all his glory rolling up to get my daughter, and there we all were ... together ... in my driveway. I wanted to die or find a very large rock to crawl under, whichever came first.

This nightmare moment of the reality of my life is so bad, even he who lacks all empathy toward me feels sorry for me. He feels so sorry for me, he actually gets out of his truck and comes to my sidewalk instead of sitting in it and waiting for me to approach as usual. "Welcome to my driveway! It's the convention of the freaking exes!" I say to him under my breath as I hand him my daughter's suitcase.

He takes our daughter's bag and says, "I'm sorry."

Wow. There is still a heart in there.

I turn around and march myself into my house, close the door, and begin another crying/questioning, "Why? Why? Why?" session for a few minutes. It's a horrible, snotty, Kleenex-flying-until-you-empty-the-box-and-head-for-the-nearest-toilet-paper-roll kind of crying. The reality of what my life has come to feels like too much weight to bear. The reality is, divorce just sucks. It sucks all the way around. You will cry until you don't, and trust me, one day, you won't cry anymore. Mostly you'll stop crying one day because he doesn't deserve the tears and because you'll be smarter than to waste any more of your precious energy on a man who isn't worth the dehydration, puffy eyes and having to give up wearing mascara.

Over the past twelve months, and the past four months since my divorce was final, I have come to see divorce in a new light. It is loss. It is grief. You don't just "get over it." You have to go through it and the accompanying emotions or you are doing yourself a great injustice. Denial is not your friend, but it may be where you are right now, and that's okay. It's where I was for quite a while. I did not want a divorce and accepting so much that was completely outside of my control was brutally painful.

I don't know where you are in the process but accepting where you are and being patient with yourself is the kindest thing you can do. Whether it's finding yourself doing the 1st, 3rd, and 5th weekend tango with two exes in your driveway or feeling stuck in the sadness of the loss, remember you are not alone. It feels that way when you are in the middle of a divorce, but don't believe those feelings. Just because your fairy tale ended badly, it's not the end of you. You don't imagine yourself as a little girl ending up in this horror scene.

You imagine yourself more like a Disney princess with the happy ending, and instead you end up looking like the scene in Cinderella where the wicked stepsisters rip her pretty, pink dress the sweet little chirping birds and squeaky mice sewed together. They worked so hard to try and build something lovely, and in an instant, it was reduced to nothing but rags.

It didn't start out that way, of course, but it ended in an ugly scene. So here you sit, at the foot of the steps of your make-believe castle, your idea of what you thought your relationship and your marriage would look like, and you stare at the mess you are in. Your make up is ruined, mascara running all over the place like a Tammy Faye Bakker flashback. Your pride is gone. Your ego is badly bruised, and you ask yourself, "How in the hell did I get here?"

This is when you wish for a fairy godmother to appear in "bibbity, boppity, boo" fashion with her magical wand. Maybe you have been waiting for a miracle too, wishing you could turn back the clock before it strikes midnight and the carriage turns back into a pumpkin and you're hobbling around on one high heel. The sad truth is, sometimes even a magic wand can't put some broken things back together. The happy truth is, you are going to be okay. No, you will be better than okay. This is not the end for you. This is a new beginning.

Now is the time to toss the fairy tale in the trash can and pick up your pen. It's time for you to write your own story. It's a new one, and it's better than the one in the trash heap. It has an amazing heroine in it, and that's *you*. *You* are holding the pen. *You* have the power. *You* do.

Please don't sit there in your tattered dress and running mascara forever. You don't need to be Cinderella anymore. This is real life, and you are capable of living it standing on your own two feet … in comfortable shoes, not those high heel glass slippers. Forget that. Forget the glass slippers! You have things to do, and those slippers are only going to slow you down. After all, there is an entire world of joy, happiness, and love ahead of you, and you need to *run*, not walk, *run* toward *that*. That man you ran toward with your arms wide open that you hoped would pick you up off your feet and spin you around just drop-kicked you off the castle balcony. Girl, he's gone, and you are going to need to start building your own kingdom -- or would it be a Queendom? Regardless, that's what needs to happen next. The time for sitting there in that torn-up gown looking like Rocky Raccoon in a prom dress is over. You must keep going no matter how you feel.

Keep taking one step forward at a time. Eventually, you will look back and feel sorry for poor Cinderella and the state she was in, but you won't *be* her anymore. You will be something better. You will be "Wonder Woman."

So forget that stupid wedding dress and the charming Prince she married even though she barely knew him. You are smarter than that now. You are strong enough to fight your own battles, and you are going to kick ass. You have so much confidence. You don't need all that lace and ribbon. Just toss you a shiny red and blue body suit and your golden power bracelets and you're good to go. Not only will you rescue yourself out of the bullshit divorce inevitably brings with it, you will bring other people with you. You will help them believe in themselves again too.

So, life and love didn't turn out the way you expected. Maybe you blame yourself, and maybe you even deserve half of the blame. Maybe you don't. Either way, it doesn't matter now. What matters it what is ahead for you. Believe this … One day you will wake up, and the pain will not hit you like a heavy weight on your heart. One day, the happiness will return and overcome that pervasive feeling of sadness. One day, you will move on. For now, here we are, and we let go and accept ourselves for the works in progress that we are. Some days you will feel strong. Some days you will feel weak. It's just the nature of the beast of a relationship ending.

We are beautiful, and where we are now is not the end. Where we are now is standing on the shore of a sea of infinite possibilities, in our Wonder Woman outfit and practical shoes, of course. Let the waves come. Guess what? You can't stop them. Be where you are. In the middle of the pain there is opportunity for personal and spiritual growth. Even though there's a lot of noise and crashing, if you listen closely it sounds like peace rolling towards you. Take heart. It's on its way to where you are.

BARE, NAKED RING FINGER

My ring finger on my left hand feels oddly naked, like it forgot to put on its bra and mascara before it left the house. It just doesn't feel right. If a finger had feelings, well I think I would say my ring finger feels vulnerable. In the days after I found out about my husband's girlfriend and he filed for divorce, I was furious ... middle-finger furious. Lately, though, I've had more ring-finger moments, the vulnerable moments. When something is vulnerable, it's susceptible to being hurt, unprotected, and in need of special care. That's the dictionary definition, and that's how I have felt much of the time since my marriage ended. I'm not a fan of feeling ring-finger vulnerable. That feeling is much more challenging to work through than middle-finger furious. As imperfect as our marriage was, my husband made me feel protected. There was safety and security. My wedding ring symbolized that I had not only a husband, but a defender. Now, all of that is gone, and the symbol of that security is hidden away in my closet where it won't remind me of all that I lost.

That left ring finger knows something is missing. It's been six months since my divorce was final. You would think that after that long, it wouldn't feel quite so strange without my wedding rings on it, but it does. I myself feel pretty naked lately, like a part of me has gone missing and needs to be placed on the side of a milk carton for hopes of finding and bringing it back home to safety. But that would be useless because the part of me that's gone missing is gone forever. The part of me that was my other half has left and joined the circus, albeit as a complete clown, and is never to return!

My rings, however, are sitting on the top shelf in my closet in a shoe box. I know that's probably not the most secure place, but I have this theory that if thieves break in, they probably won't take my shoes, especially the ones in the Payless boxes. (BOGO, ya'll.) Anyway, the thought of selling the rings, as my ex suggested way before our divorce was even final, made everything seem too real. I wasn't ready for it to be over like he was, and selling my rings seemed like a very premature move. I was holding on to more than just those rings. I was holding on for dear life, and I simply was not ready to let go -- of him, of us, of our family, of our past, of our future, of our love. I knew, as faded as it was in his heart, that the love was still there. I wasn't ready to let go of the hope that it could be rekindled.

I didn't look at my rings and see a price tag. I looked at my rings and saw a marriage and a promise smashed all to pieces. Looking at them made me want to curl up in a fetal position or bury myself underneath my bedspread for a good cry, and many days I did just that. The day I took them off my finger held the exact opposite feelings of the first day my ex put them on me.

You never forget that moment of the proposal. That beautiful ring didn't start out its journey in a shoe box. It started with a little blue box and a man on bended knee. It started with so much love and joy. It started with so much hope. I thought I had found my soul mate. I thought this time, things would be different. Now, I don't know how I could have been so wrong. In that beautiful beginning that started with these rings, I never could have imagined how things would end. They ended so badly, and he moved on so quickly. How could someone who appeared to love me so passionately all of a sudden despise me with equal intensity? How could the man who was my best friend, the person I was closest to in the world in spite of our imperfections and struggles, treat me as if I were his enemy? How could this beautiful diamond ring he gave me as a token of his love and commitment bring so much joy and now bring so much pain? I couldn't bear to look at it, but I couldn't bear to part with it, either.

My ex-husband made a point to remind me what he paid for my rings in several of our heated exchanges between my finding out about his girlfriend and our divorce being finalized. He reminded me how much he had spent on my rings and suggested I could sell them, get a nice chunk of change, and take myself on a "really nice vacation somewhere." Gee, thanks for the advice. I had a mind to tell him exactly where he could go too, somewhere nice and warm -- no, really, really freaking hot.

I loved my engagement and wedding rings. They were beautiful. What I loved even more though, was what they meant, at least at one time. I remember him sitting at the desk in my rental house one morning and pulling up a website with engagement rings, and I remember thinking, *Wow. This man really loves me. He loves me so much, he wants to make me his wife!* So, his bringing up how much he had spent and his suggestion to just sell them felt like another insult. After how badly he had betrayed me, to flippantly suggest that I just sell them and head off to the beach somewhere made me want to pull out that furious middle finger and wave it all up in front of his face. What a shame he wasted all that money on me, and what a pity I wasted all my love on a man who never loved me back enough to be "all in" the way I was "all in."

The point is that my rings continued to symbolize something to me; that reminder of how little his commitment meant to him simply hurt. The thought of selling my wedding rings wasn't something I was ready to face until much later. I certainly didn't want to break down crying in the middle of a jewelry store. I really didn't want to subject anyone to a live-action cry fest, so I figured it was better to wait until I wasn't so emotional. For a while, before I found the card from the other woman my husband was seeing and forgot to tell me about, I had hoped that maybe one day, I could wear them again. I had hoped for reconciliation and restoration of our marriage. I know now I will never have a need for those rings again. The reality is, it's hard to know what to do with your rings after a divorce. It seems like a shame to have beautiful rings worth $18,000 sitting in a shoe box in your closet, especially when most of us have attorney fees to pay, are now down to one income, may have had to move and set up a completely new home, and in general are trying to recover from the financial repercussions of a divorce. I had mostly been a stay-at-home mom for the seven years we were together, and I walked away with two thousand dollars in the bank, three thousand dollars' worth of credit card debt, and zero jobs. Once I was far enough along in my divorce recovery process, I could see that letting them go could be beneficial in more ways than one. Once I decided to go ahead and sell them, I discovered that it wasn't that easy.

Some people suggested that I keep them, but I simply see no reason to do that. To me they just symbolize pain, disappointment and rejection, and those are three things I'm determined to kick to the curb as soon as is humanly possible. My wedding rings are a painful reminder of the vows my husband chose to break. He has rationalized with timing and half-truths how this was somehow okay, but to me it felt like the furthest thing from okay and most days still does. I guess it doesn't really matter now. The most painfully clear fact is that it really doesn't matter to him. I no longer matter to him. What's done is done, and my job now is to move on. I so want to move on. If there was a "move on" button like the "easy button" from those Staples commercials, I would be all over that. Moving on isn't easy for me right now, when I'm in the middle of it. I feel stuck some days. I have moments that seem surreal, like I'm standing outside of my body looking in at my life, wondering who this strange, sad, insecure woman is. Sometimes the thought will appear like, "How did I even get here? Is this really my life?"

So, two weeks ago, I had my rings appraised at a local jewelry store. I did a lot of research related to appraisals. I had heard stories about jewelers switching out diamonds, so I wanted to have my appraisal done on the spot where I didn't have to leave my ring with anyone. After reading a lot of reviews on Yelp, I settled on a reputable local jewelry store and called them. It turned out they have a gemologist come to their store once a month to do appraisals while you wait, and you leave with your appraisal in hand. I made the appointment and marked it on my calendar. I tried to shine the grime off my rings the best I could and found a little black box to place them in before I headed off to meet the gemologist who would evaluate them and tell me exactly what they were worth. He would place this stone and steel, brilliantly and artistically crafted into rings of promise and potential, under his microscope to examine their cut and their quality. Using his special microscope, he would be able to see every ounce of beauty and worth as well as any flaw or defect hidden to the untrained and limited, naked eye. If only I could have seen things with such clarity before now. If only I had some internal X-ray machine to get a clear picture of what I was getting myself into at the time I said, "yes" at the romantic first appearance these rings made in my life so many years ago.

The gemologist informed me that if I were to take my rings to a retailer, I would likely only get twenty to thirty percent of their value. According to him, this is the absolute worst way to sell your wedding rings. So, for my $18,000 ring, if he was correct, that means I could expect to get somewhere between $3600 and $5400. I learned that a used wedding ring is worth only a small fraction of its original value. I felt a lot like that while sitting in the waiting area watching this expert size up my ring.

How are people going to size me up now? I wondered. *Here I am- "divorced twice, forty-one years old, a teacher, three kids, living on my parent's land in my grandparents' old home. No one is going to want me.*

I felt like I, too, was worth only a fraction of the value I had been twenty years prior, before I made the decision to get married in the first place. I had managed to produce two failed marriages, and the only bright spot I could see were the three beautiful children who came out of it all. All these thoughts raced through my mind as I waited for the appraiser to finish the paperwork. I had never felt more alone, sitting in that jewelry store full of beautiful rings, bracelets, and earrings carefully polished and displayed, just waiting for someone to take one home to the person they love. Sitting in that brown leather chair, I had never felt more unloved or out of place. This was a place where dreamers came who still believed in love, and weddings, and I do's and happily ever afters. In that moment, I didn't believe in any of those things anymore, and the sadness swept over me again, burning in my heart like the hot, south Texas summer air that hit me as soon as I exited the jewelry store. I wanted to go home, put my rings back in the shoe box in my closet and try not to think about them anymore. Unfortunately, I had to go meet my ex-husband to sign a passport application for him to be able to take our daughter overseas to Ireland for two weeks to visit his family. I tried to put on a brave face and shove the emotions I was feeling from the effects of the ring appraisal as far down as I could, so he wouldn't see a hint of the hurt raging like a wildfire in my heart.

I pulled up to the Fed Ex building where we were meeting and saw his truck. My adrenaline always kicked in whenever I had to see him in person, and I dreaded the fact that this wasn't a quick exchange of our daughter but instead involved paperwork forcing me to be in his presence for several minutes. He had requested to take our daughter with him to visit his family in Ireland, and he needed a signature from me. Now it was only if he needed something from me that he bothered to communicate at all. It was as if I didn't exist, except for the unfortunate occasions he had to acknowledge that I, in reality, did exist seeing as we have a child together. How annoying for him, right? Anyway, it was rare that I saw him at all anymore, but when I did, a rush of sadness and anger would well up inside of me, and I hated how that felt. It made me feel overwhelmed and vulnerable to be in the same room as him. I was going to be getting my ring appraised near where he was going to be that afternoon, so I told him I would meet him after my appointment at the jewelers. I don't know why I told him exactly. Maybe I wanted him to feel guilty, or maybe I wanted to see if he even cared. Either way, it was a mistake to bring it up. It was a mistake because it was crystal clear the man didn't give one second of thought to any feelings of guilt or remorse. Zero. All I had done was set myself up for another insult. I met him, signed what I needed to sign, and we were heading out of the door. It was all I could do to keep my mouth from saying what was in my heart. I just needed to make it a few more steps to my car, where I would cry like a pathetic baby for a few minutes before getting a grip on myself. I was so close to making it out of there with my mouth shut, but he just had to ask. "So, what did your rings appraise for?" He asked nonchalantly. He said it so casually. He said he was curious if he really had gotten a "good deal or not."

"Seriously?" I chuckled, "I guess you should have just gotten one out of a Cracker Jack Box. You could have really saved yourself a lot of money then, seeing as that's about how much they meant to you." He laughed off my comment, and I made a swift retreat toward my car, wishing I was better at hiding how upset he still made me.

Did it cross his mind, I wonder, that maybe the idea of having to get my wedding rings appraised, the rings he gave me when he promised to love and cherish me, was difficult for me? How come all he cared about was if he had "really gotten a good deal?" I don't think it crossed his mind at all that for me, the thought of selling my wedding rings was difficult, emotional, and yet another goodbye. Maybe not everyone gets attached like I do, but they were my wedding rings. When you wear something every single day of your life for approximately 2,400 days, you get a little used to them. How he was only interested in knowing if he really got a good deal seemed calloused, but there wasn't anything new about that. Some days it felt to me like he got pleasure out of hurting me or getting any kind of an emotional response from me.

The reality is, I am the one who got the really bad deal. I got royally ripped off with those rings. Those rings told me he loved me, and in the moments I couldn't feel any love from him, they were a reminder that he chose me. Until, one day, he didn't choose me anymore. He chose someone else, and those rings suddenly lost all value. To him, they meant nothing. To me, they meant something. They meant a lot when he gave them to me. I guess that was always the problem. I was always the one who cared more. So perhaps it was only fitting that the symbol of that commitment would mean nothing more to him than a business transaction, a black and white number, a pat on the back that he had "gotten a good deal." A better man would have just kept silent. A better man would have said, "I'm sorry that I hurt you." A bigger man would have said, "I'm sorry I broke the promises I made when I put those rings on your finger, and I'm sorry I broke your heart."

PAPER TRAIL OF TEARS

Today I would like to make a confession. I have cried on the phone to complete strangers this past year… *complete strangers.* I'd like to say this happened only once, but I would be lying. Let's just say I have a whole new appreciation for honesty at this point. To be more exact, these complete strangers were customer service representatives. Yes, that's really what I said … *customer service representatives,* people. It's embarrassing, I know. I realize I am grieving, and some days, the grief seems to know no boundaries. It is so inappropriate sometimes.

This probably wasn't in their job description -- listening to weepy, 40ish year old, divorcing women breaking down over a change of address. This probably sounds crazy to you, unless you have been divorced and have had to deal with not only the emotional upheaval but the financial and practical side of the unraveling of your marriage. You know that saying, "The devil is in the details?" Now, I get it.

In the wake of the separation and pending divorce, I have spoken to more customer service representatives the past several months for credit card companies, cable and internet providers, insurance agencies, and other companies you do business with trying to be a responsible adult, than I can count. For those whom were once joint "checkinged" together have now been torn asunder, and somebody has got to make the phone calls to the bank. Since I was always the responsible one who took care of all of those pesky logistics and life details during my marriage, I guess I am automatically nominated to continue that responsibility now that it's ending.

I know what you're thinking. You're probably thinking, *That's just weird, lady. You bust out crying on the phone with your insurance agent?* Or maybe you're thinking, *You really should talk to a professional, like a professional counselor. They have people for just this sort of thing, you know?* I know. Trust me. I know. I've cried to one of those people too, the professional listener. The therapists. As a matter of fact, maybe companies should start hiring counselors to take calls from all of the divorced people on the planet having to change their addresses and separate their married lives that once lived on paper.

You have a life on paper. You really do. Now all the paper has got to go to two different places, and well, somebody's got to let these people know. The lawyers don't handle all the dirty details. Many of those nasty, little details are all up to you to handle. So, in the middle of your complicated grief, welcome to the paper trail of tears. Welcome to the world of automatons welcoming you and calmly telling you to press a number or hold the line for the unsuspecting customer service representative about to be privy to the short version of, "Welcome to my personal divorce nightmare." Welcome to the awesome music you are going to get to listen to while you wait on hold for the next available representative. Welcome to getting accidentally disconnected and having to start all over again.

Every call I made felt like a small death, and with each one my heart waved another farewell to the way things were, to the way I *thought* they *should be*. I never thought I would have to do another change of address until I was old and gray and moving to a condo on some beach in Florida. Every call I had to make to straighten out where my mail was being sent made it all feel so very real. It was over. It was really over, and I would not be moving back into my home. Not only was I not moving back, he had already moved another woman in with him.

There wasn't going to be any reconciliation. My ex-husband had a girlfriend, and he was moving her into what once had been our home, my home. There was no turning back. This little brick house built by my grandparents in 1971 *was* home now.

Every time I gave my new address or took my name off an account, it felt like another little death. Each one was a reminder that my marriage was over and the home I had worked so hard to keep together was just an address to me now. That address had been mine since July of 2010 when we got engaged there in our living room. It was supposed to be our "forever home," and now it was over. There was no forever. There was only tears and paperwork … a whole hell of a lot of paperwork.

Some of it I avoided. The envelopes stacked in a pile on the corner of my desk stared at me for weeks. I knew I had to do it, especially now that someone else was moving in with my not yet ex-husband. He had been bringing me my mail in grocery bags periodically when he came to pick up our daughter. I knew I had to make the calls, but every time I made one, as hard as I tried to fight them back, the tears would come.

My call to USAA was the worst. I couldn't just ask for a change of address, I had to explain that I was getting a divorce and wanted to see if I could continue using them as my car insurance provider, even though I was not a military veteran. So, when the stranger on the other end of the line asked me what she could help me with, I took a deep breath and started to speak. The word seemed to get stuck in my throat … *divorce.* Just saying it out loud, *"My husband and I are getting a divorce,"* overwhelmed me with emotion. My voice cracked. "I'm so sorry," I told the lady on the other end of the line. "It's okay. I completely understand. We have a specific person for you to speak with who specializes in customers who are divorcing." She transferred me over, and they helped me pick my own insurance plan in my name.

There were so many changes that had to be made, and I felt like I was barely surviving. At tmes, dealing with the paperwork felt too overwhelming. There was the cell phone account that needed separating, car insurance, the cable bill was in my name, my driver's license needed updating with my new address as well as my gas card, bank card, Dillard's card, and my credit card. There was mail from my church, the pediatrician's office, my dentist's office, my kids' doctor's office, the orthodontist, the company that delivered my haircare products, my Beachbody protein shakes, my alumni letters from Texas A&M, and more I'm sure I've forgotten about, in the bags my husband brought over. Every envelope represented another phone call I needed to make.

Then there was the paperwork for my kids at school. We had moved, and with a new job where I had to leave the house at 6:00 a.m., I had to get the kids into the transportation system and on a bus route for their schools. More calls. More paperwork. More reality.

It felt never ending, until one day, I looked at the corner of my desk, and the stack was cleared away. I was finally able to move the big, alphabetized accordion folder off the kitchen table where it had made its permanent home for a few months and into the closet. I had made it to the end of the divorce paper trail. It does come to an end. The exciting thing about coming to the end of the paper trail is there are new roads for you to travel now. These roads hold the hope of possibility. These roads are an opportunity to make new discoveries about yourself, and the beautiful part is you get to choose your own path. All of the time and energy you have spent dealing with your divorce and the time-consuming and painful details that accompany it, can now be directed toward things that are positive instead of that big-ass stack of paperwork. There are new trails for you to blaze. There are paths ahead that you can create. Take a step, even if it's just one.

NEW BEGINNINGS

Today is December 31, 2016, and tomorrow is a new year. This year will be different. This year, I will look at the world with a heart full of hope and the wonder of expectation. I have gathered up the remnants of the past six months, the shock, the sting of betrayal, the pieces of my shattered heart broken into dangerously sharp shards of glass that scatter so far away from the place of initial impact, that you feel as if you will never be able to sweep them all up. I discovered too late that I placed my heart into the wrong hands for safe keeping, as love so often does. I gave my power away to someone who was not worthy, and my job now is to take my power back. I know this will not happen overnight. It will be a process. As much as I wish I could push some magical reset button on my heart, I know it will not be instant. It is going to take time. Just like the tortoise who kept slowly making its way toward the finish line one small step at a time, I know I will get there.

I have been slowly sweeping, a little more day by day. I have kept sweeping and praying and weeping and trusting. I know that one day the weeping will stop, and I look forward to that day. I hope it will come soon, a day without tears, but it hasn't yet. I know this is normal. I know this makes me human and means that to me, my marriage mattered. I valued it, and I mourn the fact that it is gone. I am determined not to wallow in self-pity, and yet I know the healthy path is not one of denial. I know in my heart that not allowing myself to feel this sadness and loss will only impede my progress in moving forward. I want this more than anything, to move forward, to get on with my life apart from my husband. We were a team, even if we weren't always playing our best; even if we were losing, we were still a team. Now, I'm on my own. I'm not used to playing this game of life alone, and some days, the loneliness is so real and pervasive. Some days I feel like I'm walking through a thick fog where I can't see clearly. The fog of grief could keep me stranded here, unable to move. I tell myself this feeling is only temporary. I tell myself I won't feel this way forever. When there is no one else to remind me, I tell myself to just hold on. These days, it's one day at a time.

I've started talking to God again, and I wonder why I ever stopped. When I feel like my thoughts are going to spiral downward inviting me to a pity party, I whisper a prayer. Lately, I whisper this prayer several times a day. "I trust you God. I trust you," is what I have started to speak over the sadness. I *do* trust Him. I wonder in quiet moments if I will ever be capable of trusting another man again. I wonder if I will ever even want to *try* to trust again. I think of the verses in Psalm 30 that speak of God turning our mourning into dancing and our weeping into laughter, of removing our sackcloth and replacing it with a garment of praise. How I want that garment of praise draped over my shoulders!

I go to church on Sundays, and I sing. I sing, and I cry, thankful that it's dark enough that no one will notice the tears quietly sliding down my cheeks. My heart is full of sadness, but it is also full of praise. I notice that it's only in these moments of worship I feel anything besides the grief. I even raise my hands now, well one hand. Let's not get *too* crazy just yet. Maybe I'll even work my way up to not caring what anyone thinks so much I'll get both hands up in the air, waving them around like I just don't care. I can't keep myself from lifting my hands in thankfulness and hope because I am *desperate*. I am *desperate* for God to take my heart, take my life, and take this pain away. I am desperate to feel better, to feel *normal* again. In these moments where I pour my heart out to God, I remember that I am not alone. I feel the anguish of loneliness all the time, except for in these moments. In these moments I remember I am not rejected but accepted by a God who loves me in my brokenness when I have nothing to offer but a heart that I helped destroy with my own stubborn will and short-sighted choices. I know I am the one who moved away -- not God. In these moments of worship, I am grateful God is here to welcome me back. I see now that I worshiped my husband, made him my hero, and when he left, my whole world crumbled.

I have gathered in the early morning hours at my kitchen table, my Bible open to the Psalms, my heart open to the only One I have trusted to heal it. As I gathered the shattered pieces of my life and placed them before a loving God, Spirit has never failed to take the broken mess from my open hands and replace it with perfect peace. In moments when I have failed to let the pieces go, when I have held on in stubbornness, in anger, and in wanting vindication, I have regretted it. Clenching a fistful of broken glass, well, it's just a stupid choice to make. It's human. It's understandable, but it's stupid. So, I show up, and I open my heart, and my hands, and . . .

I Let Go.

Letting go is the hardest thing I have ever done. I want to hold on to the anger. I don't want to forgive the man who betrayed me. I really don't want to forgive the other woman who helped. So, I keep sweeping up the pieces. I have them all gathered up now, most of them anyway, and the path before me is clear. I think it may finally be safe to take a step forward. There may be a few almost invisible specks of glass remaining, and I know that when I least expect it, my unsuspecting feet will find them. For a minute, it will sting again, but I am learning a new way. I will let myself feel the sting for just a moment, just long enough to acknowledge it before I release it, knowing now that I can let it pass through me, then give it over to the One, the only One who can do something with it. I can't wait to see the "something." I don't know what it will be, but I know it will be amazing and beautiful. I know God won't let anything be wasted because I know making broken things into beautiful things is Spirit's specialty.

So, I will brush that speck of broken glass away and keep walking, knowing that even though I cannot see anyone beside me, I am not alone.

I will say goodbye to the old ways of thinking and being, and I will say hello to the hope of a brighter future. This year I will secure the boundaries around my heart, mind, and life, and only allow people and things in that are safe.

This year, I will learn more fully how to "Let go, and let God," and I will watch in wonder as God performs miracles big and small in my life and in the lives of the people I love.

I will learn how to trust again.

I will learn how to love again.

The learning never stops.

"For I am about to do something new. See, I have already begun! Do you not see it? I will make a pathway through the wilderness. I will create rivers in the dry wasteland."

Isaiah 43:19

'TIS THE SEASON

Today is Saturday. It's the Saturday after Thanksgiving. It's the first Saturday after the second Thanksgiving I've spent alone since my divorce. Nothing about the holidays has been normal for me the past two years, and I'm learning there really is such a thing as a "new normal."

This my friends, is survival-mode thinking, and some of us find ourselves in moments of needing to just hang on for dear life this blessed time of year ... or is it rein deer life? See what I just did there? This is merely one holiday season survival mechanism-corny, corny, cringe worthy Christmas humor.

You're welcome.

You see, I'm trying to keep my sense of humor through these changes, and never are the changes more glaringly obvious than during the holiday season. It's like a spotlight has just been turned on and aimed directly at you, and you feel frozen, unable to move, squinting helplessly into the blinding light. Things have changed, and Thanksgiving and Christmas have a way of really driving that point painfully home. If you felt like a lonely, pathetic, middle-aged, divorced loser already, there's nothing like Thanksgiving, Christmas, and New Year's Eve as a single to make you feel even *better* about yourself!

It's holiday survival mode for the newly separated, divorced, or recently broken-up with someone, individuals. I happen to be the lucky, lucky winner of two of the aforementioned conditions, so I consider myself an expert on this topic. While I don't pretend to know everything, I have learned a few things that I hope may help other people, even one, trying to white-knuckle it through the holidays.

If you have one of these people in your life right now, I have two words for you -- have mercy. Seriously. Cut them some slack this holiday season. Oh, I have two more words for you, chocolate and wine. Bring us those. We'll need them once the Hallmark Channel kicks off its snowy, jingly, kissy-faced, season of hell we're trying to avoid. All this merry making, these Hallmark movies with their romantic, fireside cuddling scenes, the twinkling lights, the diamond jewelry commercials, the stupid mistletoe hanging around random doorways just taunting you, and the picture-perfect family holiday cards flowing in at an alarming, unstoppable rate, are all reminders that things are not what you thought they would be. You never imagined how much you would want to face palm yourself every time you hear the jewelry store jingle, "Every Kiss begins with Kay," or find out, "He went to Jared's!" You know what I want for Christmas? I want Kay and Jared to stop bragging and shut their freaking pie holes! Is that too much to ask?

Yep, the only man the kids might catch, "kissing mommy underneath the mistletoe," would be the literal Santa Claus because the only men hanging around are your relatives, and that would just be weird. So, while these idealized, romantic notions of the holiday season are warming your happily coupled hearts, just remember they can also make the people who are already alone feel like throwing a freshly baked plate of warm, gingerbread cookies right at the TV screen. Take that, Kay and Jared! Look out Candace Cameron and Tori Spelling! I've got slightly burned yet still edible holiday cookies coming in hot and headed right toward your Hallmark bliss. There might be a strong case of single, holiday depression and angst coming straight for your on- screen make-out session. So, you'd better duck and cover.

On the bright side, I have to say that this year, I feel like I'm handling this whole alone scenario like a rock star compared to last year. Now, *that* sucked. I felt like I had been run over by a Mack truck emotionally. You might as well have stopped calling me by my real name and just started referring to me as, "Flat Stanley." Where was "Flat Stanley" last Christmas season? Flat Stanley could be found sitting on the sofa in running gear, crying into an industrial-sized container of cheese balls, watching Diane Lane in "Under the Tuscan Sun" on Netflix. My heart was crushed. I was broken.

Last winter, my now ex-husband was spending his holidays with the "other woman" (to sum it up), and I was pretty much a puddle of pathetic devastation. He also introduced her to our then five-year-old on Christmas, which I was super pumped about … It was pretty bad last year. I am not going to even pretend it wasn't.

My older sister, who has become my best champion through this mess, graciously included me in their Thanksgiving. I found myself making frequent trips to the bathroom to cry just a little every few hours. I also found myself crying in the bathroom intermittently all through Christmas as well. As you can see, I spent a lot of time in bathrooms last holiday season. I choked back tears the entire Christmas Eve service at church watching families sit together. I choked back tears while I watched my brother and his family take pictures together in front of the tree on Christmas day because I didn't have my family the way I had known it anymore. Let's just refer to it as the Christmas trail of tears.

Then this past year, I met a nice man when I was out dancing with my girlfriends one night, and he asked for my number. He was cute, smart, an Aggie just like me, a great dancer, and we shared many of the same interests like theater, music, and running. He started calling me, and we started going on dinner dates. Things slowly progressed, and by the summer we were spending a lot of time together, traveling together, and he was even becoming a part of my kids' lives after several months of dating and making sure this had potential to move forward. He was great to my kids. He took the time to talk to them beyond surface-level conversations about their lives. He included them. He became my best friend, my person. You know your person, the one you call when you get in your car after work and talk to all the way home about your day and their day and all the minutia of the in-between. I had that again.

He would buy groceries, show up at my house, and cook dinner for us, or if I cooked, he would do all the dishes. When I had two places to be at the same time to pick my teenagers up from after-school activities, he was happy to help pick one of them up, since he worked from home and had a flexible schedule. He even did laundry when he came over. Read that again, people. *Laundry.* He held hands at the dinner table and led us in prayer before meals. He went to church with me on Sundays. He talked to my kids about their plans for their future, their goals, and their dreams. He played board games with my youngest in the living room while I was grading papers. I thought he was a keeper.

He had even passed the parent approval rating, no easy feat. I had met his son who lived out of the country with his mother and stepdad. I had met his mother, his father, his stepmother, friends he used to work with, attended his sister's wedding in the spring and his family reunion in September. *I was able to trust again, which I didn't think would be possible.*

I thought this season of loss had all turned around. I thought I had managed to find a good man who would be sitting next to me in church this Christmas Eve and watching the Hallmark movies with me. There would be no throwing of cookies, and maybe I wouldn't even mind Kay and Jared too much this year.

This year, I had really been looking forward to the holidays. We had already planned out Thanksgiving and Christmas. So even though last year the holidays were lonely and difficult, I had been thinking about how happy I was and how much things can turn around in a year's time. There would be no holiday blues this season.

Not this year! I thought, mentally clenching my triumphant fist high into the wintery air with the conviction matched only by the likes of William Wallace before he charged the English army at the Battle of Stirling Bridge. "This year there *will be happiness at the holidays!*"

Insert "WRONG answer" buzzer sound effect.

Did you hear it? That was the sound of my hopes of seasonal bliss being "wrong answer" buzzed into oblivion.

Funny how everything can go to hell in a hand basket with one little click of the old mouse. At the beginning of October, I was at my sister's house grading papers, and before I shut down my lap top, I decided it would be a good idea to check my email one last time. Do you remember the opening scene in, "You've Got Mail," when Meg Ryan talks about that excited feeling, that anticipation you get when you open your email and hear, "You've Got Mail!" Oh, I had mail all right, but this was not mail to get excited about. It was mail from hell.

By the time I opened my email and read all the way to the end, there was no question the sound track for my Christmas this year would be less Burl Ives, "A Holly Jolly Christmas," and more Dolly Parton, "Hard Candy Christmas."

It turned out my perfect boyfriend had another girlfriend he started dating *after me* that he accidentally forgot to mention. According to her, a very successful, not easily bamboozled litigation attorney, there were apparently other women he was somehow managing to find the time to date in between seeing us! Insert gasp and look of sheer horror. She figured it out when she kept seeing my name appear on his caller ID and rifled through his phone. Thank God, she did, or I might still be dating Sir Lies a Lot.

"Hmmm." I thought after a few days of freaking out. "There appears to be a pattern here." These men keep forgetting about these other women they have scattered about to and fro. It must be taxing on the old memory. Maybe they need some Ginkgo Biloba. Maybe, as my sister suggested, we need an all-points bulletin, "International Douchebag Alert" system. All I know is I could barely keep up with *one* boyfriend, much less *two*! I mean, where did he find the time, and how is he not an Academy Award-winning actor being able to master the craft of being so believable yet so full of complete crap?

The seemingly wonderful, attentive, successful man I thought I was in an exclusive, progressing relationship with was a big, fat-as-Santa's-bowl-full-of-jelly-belly, liar. The tangled web lying Mr. Liar Pants had been weaving all came unraveled just in time for the holiday season.

Here's the happy ending. I survived, and you will, too. Not only did I survive, I managed to find an incredible amount of joy, peace, and reconnection to God in the year and a half since my separation and divorce. I also managed to find myself and remember who I was, what I like, what I'm passionate about, and what my dreams are. I made it my mission to find healing from what I can only sum up as trauma, and I pursued that healing with focused determination as if my life depended on it ... because it did.

Jesus said he came down to this crazy world that night in Bethlehem to give us abundant life, and I am not about to settle for a broken life when I know God is the one who is able to make the broken mess something beautiful. So, here I am again, but this time, it's easier. This time, I know I survived last holiday season. I thought I would die, but I didn't. I made it through. This year there were far fewer tears and no swift emergency exits to the bathroom to shed a few tears before giving myself a mirror pep talk to get me through.

So, if you are facing this holiday season with heartache, let's look at the bright side together, shall we?

#1 It is much better to be alone at the holidays (or any time) than with the wrong person.

#2 You have one fewer present to buy. Cha-ching!

#3 You can stay in your pajamas all day, not wear any make up, eat straight out of the ice cream container, and have complete control of the remote on your holiday vacation after the kids are all in bed, and there is no one there to judge you. Can you say "awesome?"

#4 You can decorate your white Christmas tree you pick out yourself with hot pink beads and hot pink ornaments, and there's no one there to stop you.

#5 You don't have to share any of the left-over advent calendar chocolate the kids didn't want with anyone else. It's all yours. Score!

You see, there is always a silver bells lining.

"LOVE BITES"
—Def Leppard, 1987

It seems the rock bands of the '80s said it best. Yes, sometimes, love *does* bite, and it really can bring you to your knees. Thanks Def Lep for the warning back there in the '80s. If only I had listened to you in junior high, maybe I wouldn't be sitting here so jaded in 2018. You know, love really isn't all that bad. Lest you think I am incurably cynical, I know it can be pretty great. I do remember that. It's just that sometimes, well, we handle it all wrong. Sometimes we pick the wrong person in which to invest our love, and it comes back to bite you right in the ass, Def Leppard style.

One of the most annoying things anyone has said to me in the past year and a half is how it takes two to jack up a relationship and that both parties must have contributed to its demise in some way. Here's a news flash for the "it takes two" crew: you're wrong. In many instances that may be true, but sometimes, all it takes is one person to murder a relationship with their stupid decisions. Which leads me to the infinite wisdom of another '80s rock god, Jon Bon Jovi. Jon, here's a shout out to you reminding us that there are people who can simply ruin the good reputation of romantic love. I call on Bon Jovi's 1986 love gone wrong anthem, "You Give Love a Bad Name" as my expert witness that sometimes, there's only one person to blame, if you're into blaming. If you don't know the song, it says, "Shot through the heart, and you're to blame. You give love a bad name."

Speaking of biting and shooting people, this brings me to the bullet ant. Yes, I said this brings me to an *ant*. Bear with me. I'm going somewhere with this. If you don't trust '80s rock stars when it comes to their pontifications on love, I give you science! To be specific, I give you an entomologist because when love does bite you in the ass, it's amazing how difficult it can be to put into words just how agonizing it can feel.

Have you ever been stung by a fire ant? It's excruciatingly painful. Typically, you don't get stung by just one. You're usually standing in the yard, or the soccer field, or on a sidewalk, and suddenly you feel a sharp sting. By the time you realize what's happening, there's usually a small swarm of these devilish little demon insects scurrying around your ankles and between the crevices of your toes. At this point, it's too late. They are scary fast, and their bites are nasty. Being that I'm from Texas, and we have a lot of fire ants, I was curious when I came across an article at the tail end of a random Google search tangent of deadly jungle animals. It turns out there exists a species of ant even more vicious than the fire ant: the bullet ant. As you may have guessed, this evil insect's name is attributed to the fact that its sting feels like being hit by a bullet.

In the article I read, an entomologist named Dr. Justin Schmidt, invented something called the "Schmidt Sting Pain Index" that's like a rating scale of pain you feel when stung by a certain order of insects like wasps, bees, and ants. Apparently, the bullet ant reaches the pain index's highest level. Dr. Schmidt described what it felt like to be stung by this ant while he was collecting them in Brazil. In describing the pain, he writes,

"There were huge waves and crescendos of burning pain -- a tsunami of pain coming out of my finger. The tsunami would crash as they do on the beach, then recede a little bit, then crash again. It wasn't just two or three of these waves. It continued for around 12 hours. Crash. Recede. Crash. It was absolutely excruciating. There wasn't much I could do except be aware of it and groan."

As soon as I read the description of the pain this small creature inflicts, it reminded me of exactly how I would describe the pain of betrayal and divorce at the beginning stages. It felt like wave after never-ending wave of anger, sadness and despair with brief respites of calm in between. The only difference would be that the 12 hours of oscillating levels of agony following the initial sting of the bullet ant is more like a 12-month ordeal. Every time I remember my deepest feelings of pain in the immediate fallout after realizing my marriage was over, I see a few visual images run through the movie reel of my mind.

The first image I see is my ex-husband's red, metal upright tool chest in the garage and me standing in front of it holding the lipstick stained envelope with his name on it, reading the card from his lover. Like an out-of-body experience, I see the absolute shock and horror of the words I'm reading wash over my face. I remember feeling paralyzed with disbelief, especially when I saw the name signed at the closing of the card. It felt like the world slowed down in that moment, and all I could hear was the beating of my heart, pounding so frantically from the adrenaline I could hear it in my ears. I see myself four days later sitting at my desk in my classroom, listening to a message left on my cell phone from my husband's attorney. I remember thinking how feigned his apology rang of how "sorry" he was and that he was calling to let me know my husband had filed for divorce. There are many other images I see in my mind like a collage of moments where the waves would crash so relentlessly against my heart I feared I would drown. There were moments I would have *liked* to have drowned just to make the pain stop.

What I would have liked to have heard in the middle of the emotional "tsunami" is that the pain will eventually recede, and the waves will stop crashing. They *will* stop crashing. There also comes a day where you stand on the shoreline of your life and make a choice to head for higher ground when you see the tides start to pick up again. Unfortunately, I didn't have the luxury of being able to completely break contact with my ex, which made the heading for higher ground difficult. That would have made the ending exponentially easier. There were triggers that would bring on the waves, and all I could do was try to orchestrate avoidance to the best of my ability.

I still had to see him when he picked up our daughter, and worse, I had to see him with his new girlfriend. I had to communicate with him regarding the logistics of the custody agreement, and he didn't make that easy on any level. What I tried to avoid was going anywhere near my old house. If any one thing summoned the crashing of waves on the shore of my heart again, it was having to go to what once was my home. Driving up to the house we once lived in as a family felt like I was sticking my hand right in the middle of a mound of bullet ants. It was going to sting, and I knew it. There were times I couldn't avoid picking our daughter up at my old house, like the time my ex was supposed to bring her back to me but "couldn't find his keys." That particular day, I happened to be on my way home from watching a movie with my two oldest children, and when he called to ask me to come pick her up, they were with me. My oldest daughter hadn't been back to the house since the day she left for choir camp the previous summer, not knowing, just as I didn't know, that when I picked her up from camp, we wouldn't be returning to our home. As I pulled out of the driveway that evening after picking up my youngest daughter, I looked over at her in the passenger seat, and silent tears were streaming down her beautiful face. All I could do was tell her how sorry I was, that I loved her, and that I understood. My oldest had put on such a brave face that I had forgotten the pain had bitten her, too.

What was difficult to swallow was how my ex-husband couldn't understand, even though I had told him, that he needed to bring my daughter to me because it was too painful to drive up to that house. Maybe he did understand, and maybe he just didn't care. I started to believe that maybe he even enjoyed the fact that he still had the power to hurt me. He almost seemed to enjoy parading the girlfriend in front of me, bringing her in the car with him to pick up my daughter, sending packages signed by her to my home. Had it been a woman he had met after we had divorced who had nothing to do with the ending of our marriage, things would have been very different. However, this woman was at the center of the end of it all, and my ex expected me to accept and respect her. It was insulting.

The fact that I had to watch another woman walk into what I had once made a home for my family was agonizing. If pulling up to your old house, seeing the climbing honeysuckle vines you resurrected from near death and nurtured until they cascaded like a green waterfall over your fence, the Celtic cross stained glass your English aunt gave you as a wedding gift still hanging in your kitchen window, and the rocking chair on the front porch where you used to sit and think how grateful you were for your life, and then some strange woman your husband replaced you with walk in the front door, doesn't make you feel like your life has been abducted by aliens, you would have to be a heartless robot. In the end, it was the thoughtless discard and the swift replacement that stung the worst.

Then one day, I woke up and realized the grief had lifted off my heart to the point where I felt physically lighter. The shoreline of my heart was still, with only the faint sound of gentle, rolling waves approaching. I knew that the tides had changed. I knew that I was healing.

While I don't believe I will ever forget the pain of the sting of betrayal and divorce, I do believe time, prayer, meditation, and love have and will continue to heal the wound. My first questions a year and a half ago were simply why and how. Why is this happening and how did I end up here? After the first six months I started asking a different "how." How can I forgive so that I can let go? That was the toughest question to answer and the one I have struggled with the most. The question then changed from why to what now? How do I take what I learned from the pain and transform it into a lesson? What have I learned about myself? What have I learned about life and about love? What have I learned about letting go? Most importantly, I started asking myself how can I live fully in this present moment where I see my past as only thoughts and my future as only thoughts? In other words, how can I live where not a moment of my time is wasted looking back or worrying about what is to come?

While I don't know all the answers, I do know that it has been in the silent moments of meditation while I read and prayed that I found the most peace. I do know that I only had to travel as far as my back-yard view of the pasture, the trees, the birds, and the sound of the wind to realize I could find peace in sitting in the stillness of a moment. Divorce taught me that I don't need very much to be truly happy. Divorce taught me that true happiness is being connected to God and making yourself available and willing to follow the Holy Spirit's lead. Divorce taught me that when I keep my heart tied closely to God, there is no way I could wander where I should not go. Divorce taught me that it is never too late to begin again and that God can use our failures and pain to breathe purpose and passion into our dead hearts. Divorce taught me how to love again, starting with loving myself.

So, while romantic love may bite some of us in the ass at some point, there is a love that really does always protect, always defend and never, ever ends. If nothing else, divorce taught me that God's love for me and for all of us is the safest love we could ever know. Romantic love will fail you. It will disappoint you. It will leave you writhing in agony from the sting of being let down. The good news is, you'll live. The good news is your life can be even better than it ever was before. I had to lose everything to be reminded of what love really is. True Love won't trade you in for something shiny and new. True Love won't reject you and replace you. True Love is the father, watching for you, waiting to see you appear over the horizon in the distance, running to you with his arms open wide to greet you. Love, true Love is alive, and it's there for every single one of us. True Love doesn't bite. True Love invites. It invites you to come, exactly as you are, and stay forever.

STUPID TREE

I love Shel Silverstein. He was responsible for my first real relationship with books. You see, I fell in love with his writing when I was nine years old. My friend, Erin, whose mom was also my teacher, started reading his book, *Where the Sidewalk Ends,* in third grade. She brought it to school for show and tell, and after looking at his illustrations and belly laughing with my friends at some of his poems, I knew I needed his poetry in my life. I begged my mom to buy it for me, and she did. I thought it was the best thing I had ever heard read aloud. Erin's mom was my third-grade language-arts teacher, Mrs. Rich (an oxymoron of a surname for a teacher, as I now know firsthand). Mrs. Rich had a great sense of humor, and she would often read Shel Silverstein out loud to us.

Mrs. Rich was calm, never raised her voice, and had the best read-aloud voice of any teacher ever in the history of all teachers. She was my favorite teacher because I could tell that she loved books and enjoyed what she did. She was smart. She knew that if she could get us laughing and engaged with a book, we would fall in love with reading. I don't know about everyone in the class, but I know I did. *Where the Sidewalk Ends* began my first love relationship with a piece of writing. I fell in love with words and ideas. I fell in love with the magical quality of being able to sit in my little bedroom way out in the middle of nowhere on our cattle ranch and be transported to a completely different place and time.

That book of poetry was the first book I ever asked for. The illustrations were intriguing. The poems were hilarious. I memorized, "Sick," and "One Sister for Sale." I read "Jimmy Jet and his TV Set" and could just imagine little Jimmy growing an electrical cord tail out of his rear end and being plugged into the wall to be watched by his whole family. Shel Silverstein made me laugh. His writing was silly and funny, and his imagination inspired me to imagine that maybe one day, I could write poetry, too. I connected with this book, and like all good books, it helped shape a small part of who I am. It inspired me to imagine and think outside the box. It showed me that books didn't always have to be serious. They could make you laugh, and we all know that laughter is good medicine for the heart and soul. I think I took myself pretty seriously, even as a kid, so Mr. Silverstein helped me learn how to lighten up a little.

Then one day many years later, I saw a book called *The Giving Tree* by Shel Silverstein. So of course, I knew I needed to read it. When I finally got hold of a copy, it was not what I expected. This book was not funny. It was deep. It was profound. It was serious. It made me feel something inside, the way a good writer makes a reader feel and think and see the world in a different way. This was a different Shel Silverstein. Before I actually read the book for myself, I heard a lot about it. If I ever mentioned Shel Silverstein, inevitably I would hear, *Oh! Have you read The Giving Tree?* I kept hearing that *The Giving Tree* was a wonderful children's book, so when I read it, I thought, "What? This is sad, and I'm having a lot of mixed feelings right now about the message!" It was not what I expected.

I had heard it was about selflessness and unconditional love, but after reading it, I didn't agree with that interpretation at all. Yes, the tree was selfless and loved the boy unconditionally, but as I finished reading it I was more disturbed at the boy's selfish behavior. I mean, he never even says, "Thanks, tree, for chopping off all your lovely limbs and ending up a freaking stump!" All I could think was, "What the heck is your problem, kid? Can't a tree get a little bit of appreciation?" The boy grows and turns into a man, and he never seems to learn to appreciate the tree. He just keeps coming back and taking.

Boy, can I relate to the tree. I can really relate to the tree. You see where I'm going with this don't you? Funny, I had no idea writing about Shel Silverstein would lead me right back to my original thesis of this book, also known as, "My ex-husband was a selfish, egocentric jerk who threw me away faster than an empty can of Bud Light." I'm almost certain if he shows back up as an old man, he would find my stump a useful coaster for a double vodka tonic. The sad thing is, I would have kept giving just like old girl, Giving Tree. G.T.

was selfless, and it destroyed her. The scary part is, it says she was happy when he came back and sat on her to rest.

I guess some people just want to be useful. Maybe some people get so used to being used they lose all sense of their identity. The tree existed to give and wasn't happy if she wasn't fulfilling that role. I think the tree was an empath, and the boy was a narcissist. He seemed to have a sense of entitlement and no regard for her feelings. He took advantage of the giving nature of the tree to get what he wanted, regardless of how it affected her. As you can see, *my* current interpretation is this guy is a narcissistic jackass. *The Giving Tree* taught me that indeed, no matter how much you love someone and give everything you can for someone out of pure intent, there are just some people who don't know how to love you back and will never change. The behavior of the boy/man/old man didn't have anything to do with the value of the tree. The tree didn't do anything wrong except love the wrong kind of boy, the kind that only knows how to take.

IN A JAR WITH JESUS

L ater on down the road, I stumbled across a copy of
another one of Shel Silverstein's books called *The
Missing Piece*. I had never heard of this book, so I
started reading it with zero background knowledge. I remember how I felt as the realization of the profound and complex
message wrapped in the simplicity of his illustrations began
to sink in. In *The Missing Piece*, the character, a pie-shaped
wedge, the "missing piece," is sitting all alone waiting for a
circle to come along where it can fit in and roll along together.
It is a wedge, after all and doesn't think it can roll on its own.

Various shapes come by and the missing piece attaches itself
to them. They roll along for a while, but they are always the
wrong fit, and in the end it just doesn't work out. They always
end up going their separate ways. Then one day a circle comes
along with the exact fit for the wedge. They roll along until
the wedge begins to grow, and grow, and eventually outgrows
the circle. Finally, a new character, the Big O, comes along.
The Big O isn't missing anything. The missing piece tells the

Big O it's the one he/she has been looking for. The Big O explains to the wedge that while the wedge cannot roll with him, maybe it could roll along beside The Big O. The wedge isn't so sure how to do this. As a matter of fact, the wedge doesn't even know if it is possible. It has never even thought to try it before. The wedge begins to express all the seemingly obvious and logical reasons it cannot roll by itself. The wedge is full of excuses. The wedge has a helpless mentality.

"But I have sharp corners," and "I am not shaped for rolling," the wedge tells the Big O. The Big O leaves, and the wedge has what Oprah would call an, "Ah Ha!" moment. The wedge lifts itself up onto one corner and begins to flop and plop itself over and over again until something magical happens. The corners begin to wear off, and the wedge begins to transform itself. The wedge transforms itself with its sheer determination. The missing piece had to decide that it was done making excuses as to why it could not move by itself and simply decided to try. With sheer determination and some encouragement by a wiser Big O, the missing piece discovers there is something else possible besides helplessly sitting and waiting.

I picked this book up at a time when I knew I had become co-dependent in my relationship with my husband. I was so busy trying to fix him, save him, and save our marriage, that I lost myself. I felt helpless much of the time because when it comes to trying to control the choices and actions of someone else, you *are* helpless. I was in the process of trying to learn how to let go. I was in the process of learning that the only person I could be responsible for and control was myself. I worked so much on myself in counseling to be able to stay sane in the midst of the constant chaos my husband's actions and choices created, that I was becoming a different person. In order to survive, I had to.

This book, *The Missing Piece*, taught me that sometimes you just may need someone to roll beside you and remind you that something new, a new way of being, is possible. Change is possible. Transformation is possible, even if it's one ungraceful, ugly plop-and-flop flounder at a time. The corners of the wedge wore off until the wedge was no longer a helpless, static triangle but a dynamic, rolling circle. In the end, the wedge (now the circle) catches up to the Big O, and the last scene of the book is them rolling along together. What a beautiful allegory for love and transformation. Originally when I read it, my hope was that my husband and I would be able to roll along side by side one day. Now, I am learning that I am not helpless. I am learning that I can be alone, and that I am capable of taking care of myself. I am learning to stop making excuses and to replace that with action. Yes, sometimes I feel like I'm plopping and flopping. Eventually, I hope my sharp edges will wear off as well, and I will be able to move through this beautiful universe the way I am meant to travel -- on track, on time, and on purpose.

I felt a lot like that little wedge this past year. Some days I didn't want to move at all. Sometimes it seems so much easier just to stay exactly where you are. Stuck is comfortable. If you are stuck in one place long enough, even a terrible place, that place can start to feel like home. Thank God for the Big O's of the world. Thank God for them.

I had a couple of Big O's come along while I was going through my divorce, feeling like my life was over and I would die, a sad, lonely wedge. I did have one advantage over the little wedge in Shel Silverstein's story. I had a cell phone and the power of Google.

In December of 2016 I had been given the date of the final hearing for my divorce. I knew that the day my divorce was final would hit me hard emotionally. How could it not? It would be officially over, and I would have to learn how to accept it. I knew it was going to be difficult, and I decided to do some research to see if there were any retreats around that time that dealt with healing from a divorce.

One of the places I researched caught my attention. I continued to search for other retreats, but I kept coming back to one particular place, the Crystal Bay Hotel in St. Petersburg, Florida. They were holding a "Life Lessons Weekend Retreat," and the description sounded like it perfectly matched what I was looking for. The price was very reasonable; in fact, it seemed so reasonable I decided to call the hotel to inquire about the cost and what was included in the price. That call introduced me to Pat, who was the manager of the hotel. He was so kind as I explained to him my reason for wanting to attend the retreat. "I can't think of a better place for you to be right after the final hearing of your divorce," he said. "The last thing you want is to repeat any patterns in your future relationships," he continued, "and Dr. Tong is excellent at helping you figure out what it was you were meant to learn from your relationship." Pat could not have been more spot on.

It was a divine appointment. As I learned about the seven basic spiritual life lessons we're here to learn, I discovered that I had only learned *one*: yes, *one*. That one lesson I had down was divine guidance, and I knew it was that guidance that led me to Saint Petersburg, Florida, a place I had never even heard of before until a few weeks prior. I had spent months praying for God to heal my heart and mind. When the final hearing for our divorce was scheduled for January, 2017, I knew it was going to set off another cycle of grief. Funny how grief is not a "one-and-done." Just when you think you're good, it can hit you again out of nowhere almost as fresh as when it first happened.

I had been going to counseling but usually ended up feeling just as bad, if not worse, when I left a session because I ended up crying my way through a box of Kleenex each time. I didn't really feel like it was helping. I felt stuck. I was going to a support group and spending a lot of time praying, meditating, and reading my Bible and other self-help type books on my own. I would have a few days before Christmas break was over in January, so not really knowing where to look, I Googled something like, "divorce retreat" or "healing retreat." After researching several different retreat weekends, I kept coming back to the "Life Lessons Weekend" with Dr. Mark Tong at the Crystal Bay Hotel in St. Petersburg, Florida.

The description of the retreat sounded perfect for what I was looking for. "Dr. Tong has identified 7 Spiritual 'life

lessons' that continually repeat in our lives until we have identified and learned from them. In this 'Life Lessons' healing
retreat, you will discover 'The 7 Life Lessons,' the emotions
tied to each one and various spiritual concepts to understand
the lesson and the process developed to accelerate your Spiritual
Growth. You will learn how to identify, and more importantly,
learn from the lessons so they will never repeat."

Never repeat? Yes, please! I called the number on the website and was fortunate enough to speak to the kindest soul
on the other end of the line. His name was Patrick. I asked
some questions about the retreat, the accommodations, and
the price and briefly told him the reason I was drawn to the
retreat. "There isn't a better place you could be right after
your divorce. You are going to love Dr. Tong. He's really
wonderful, and I think you will get a lot out of it." Patrick
spent several minutes just talking to me on the phone. From
the first moment of contact with the staff at Crystal Bay, I
felt comforted and encouraged. That weekend proved to be
nothing short of life-changing. Dr. Mark Tong helped me to
identify the lessons I had yet to learn, but more importantly,
helped me to re-frame my divorce. He helped me re-frame
everything, and I've never looked at anything the same. I
made a mental shift of seeing myself as a victim to someone
who was so lucky to be free from a toxic relationship. I was
able to realize that my world fell apart because I had made a
man my God. I was also starting to learn that thinking I was
"alone" was not reality. God was there, and always had been.
Feeling and thinking I was somehow separate from Source

wasn't true. All of a sudden, I knew I wasn't alone and that the past was a lesson I could learn from and move forward.

I traveled to St. Pete's, as the locals refer to it, completely heart-broken. If the condition of my soul could be labeled in hospital terms, it was in critical condition, and I was in need of life support. Compounding the deep sadness and anxiety I was feeling about the finality of the divorce, was the shocking news I had received that first week of January. My husband (we were still not officially divorced yet), emailed me that he was moving his girlfriend, the other woman, from Seattle to Texas to live in his house with him that week, the first week of January. I was absolutely dumfounded.

The pain I was feeling multiplied exponentially once I found out he was moving her into the house that we had gotten engaged in, brought our daughter home to, and lived in together. I was being replaced, and his relationship with this woman I despised was moving to a whole new level. Flashbacks of his words, "Baby, I could never find another girl like you. I could never replace you," echoed in my thoughts. He *had* found someone else. He *had* replaced me, and I felt like a disposable plastic tablecloth at the end of a barbecue picnic. My relationship with my husband had left me a stained, awful mess, and instead of him being willing to correct his behavior and mistakes and put in the work to fix what his choices had broken, he chose to crumple me up and toss me in the big, black Hefty garbage bag of his life. It hurt, and it hurt badly because in my heart I believed that even though we were broken, we could find healing and find our way back to each other.

When I arrived in St. Pete, the emotions were raw, and I felt fragile. I was looking for answers. I was searching for healing. I was desperately fighting to not drown in the pain. Over the past several months I had been praying for God to guide me on the right paths toward healing my heart. As much as I prayed, I had moments where I just wanted to numb out for a little bit, and at times I did. The day I decided to Google search for a retreat focused on healing after a divorce was the same day I ended up alone while the kids were with their dads. I sprawled out on my living-room couch, elbow deep into a giant jar of cheese balls and two Shiner beers, watching Tony Robbins' documentary called, "I Am Not Your Guru," sobbing in my sweaty running gear. Yes, I did run three miles and then eat half my body weight in cheese balls. As tempting as it was to numb out with food, wine, television, or any distraction I could find, I knew I needed to face the fear, sadness, and anger if I was ever going to get past the betrayal and disappointment. I slid out of bed every morning praying for God to give me strength, heal me, and help me forgive and let go. I was signed up to begin Divorce Care classes at my church and had been going to traditional counseling, but I was still struggling. Finding this retreat felt like God's perfect timing, especially after talking with Pat and hearing him explain the purpose of the retreat more fully.

Part of the retreat weekend included a fifteen-minute, one-on-one session with Dr. Mark Tong, the spiritual counselor who owned the hotel and was teaching the workshop. Little did I know that my brief time with him would catapult me further ahead in my healing journey than I thought was possible. Before the session, he had me fill out an inventory checklist that included questions about my past, including past trauma and loss. When he called me into his office and heard my story, he excused himself and went out to speak to his secretary. "I'm guessing this is such a mess you just went and asked your secretary to clear your schedule for longer than fifteen minutes, huh?" I joked upon his return. He laughed because he had done just that.

I will be forever grateful that this wonderful, gifted healer took the time, at no extra cost, to listen to my story, ask me thoughtful questions, and lead me through a very powerful guided meditation. The goal of the meditation was to help me "unplug" from my ex and to reconnect to Source, to God. Dr. Tong helped me see that I had "disconnected" from God and "plugged into," or given my power away, to my husband, who didn't deserve it. He helped me visualize cutting emotional "cords" that tied me to my past and to my husband. He had me visualize God's love and light filling my mind and heart. Part of the guided meditation was him having me imagine putting my husband in a glass jar, with holes poked in the top of course, so he could breathe. I would have preferred no holes at the time, but I guess that isn't very Zen like. Anyway, I was to screw the lid on tightly. "He can't hurt you anymore," he said. "He's in the jar. Now, imagine a beam of God's light and love flowing from your heart center and filling up the jar.

You're filling the jar up with God's love because he (the ex) is going to need it. Now imagine you are handing the jar up to Jesus, who takes the jar from your hand. It is not your job to take care of your ex anymore. It is not your job to worry about him anymore. He's with God, and God will take care of him."

I'm sure I'm not remembering his words verbatim, but it's close. This visualization helped me more than anything to be able to really begin letting go. If you're stubborn, letting go is not the easiest thing in the world to do. I had a death grip on my marriage, and this meditation allowed me to loosen my grip until my hands were palms up and open. I had felt like I was trying to pry my own fingers off the promises and hopes for a life with my husband and our marriage to no avail, and Dr. Tong's guided meditation helped me to willingly and peacefully let go.

It also helped me to accept responsibility for my part in this big mess of a divorce. I had made the choice, unconsciously, but still a choice, to "give my power away" to my husband. I alone had chosen to "unplug" from my Source. It was up to me to fix that. No one else could ever do that for me.

When I returned home, I didn't know where to begin explaining the deep healing work that had begun in my heart. I was still hurting, and I knew I would for a while, but I had a peace and had finally entered the grieving stage we call "Acceptance." For me, the "Acceptance" stage has been an on-going process, but I finally felt it was going to be possible for me to truly let go and move forward. Dr. Tong had helped me do a mental shift. That shift in perspective made all the difference. Plus, it was kind of fun summing up my session by simply stating that my soon to be ex-husband was, "In a jar with Jesus." I had handed him off to the big man upstairs, and he wasn't my problem anymore.

WATCH YOUR MOUTH

I know nothing in the world that has as much power as a word. Sometimes I write one, and I look at it until it begins to shine.

Emily Dickinson

Speaking of Fairy Godmothers and "bibbity, bop-pity, boo," I think it's important for me to tell you about someone. Her name is Florence Scovel Shinn, and she wrote a little book many years ago called, *Your Word is Your Wand.*

I came across this book one night when I was home alone in July 2016. It was right after I moved back to the ranch where I grew up, and the kids were all gone for the weekend. Over and over I kept replaying the last moments I had spent with my husband in our kitchen before he disappeared and left me a check on his desk to "pay the movers" to move our things out. I kept replaying in my mind his words that pierced my heart and changed the course of my life forever. No matter how tumultuous life was with him, I loved him, and I didn't want a life without him.

I was inconsolable. I was furious. I was confused. I was lost. My parents and closest friends insisted, "He is telling you he doesn't want you and to move out! What else were you supposed to do? You didn't have another option. It's time." After all of the crazy stunts and previous disappearing acts, the nights of not knowing where he was, who he was with, or if he was coming home, the disrespect, the disregard for me, for my feelings and for all the promises he had made when he asked me to marry him in the first place, after all of it, *he* was telling *me* to leave? My mom asked me if I had finally "had enough." My best friends, Jenny and Eric, told me it was time. I knew my family and friends were right, but all I wanted was for him to come home and tell me to come back, to tell me he loved me and had made a terrible mistake.

When he finally did reappear, more than a week later, he called me from an emergency room in a hospital in Virginia Beach telling me he had chest pains and had come into the ER. It was the first time I heard his voice in eight days. He told me he would go to rehab. He told me he had a friend who was going to AA and said he would start going with him. He sounded remorseful. He agreed to go to counseling with me. He texted me that it would be hard, but we could make it work. I had hope again for a moment.

A day or so later, I got a message from a neighbor telling me a different story. She informed me that my husband was telling *them* he would go to rehab, but he didn't think it would make any difference because, "Cody has anger issues and can't forgive." *Why thank you Dr. Phil for that astute assessment.* Another friend messaged me asking, "What in the world is going on?" It turns out my husband had simply told her, "Cody left me. She just packed up and moved out." So, this was his spin on kicking me out of his home and his life? It was my fault? I had "anger issues?" Well, if I didn't have anger issues before, I most definitely did in that moment of harsh realization. It was bad enough the way he was ending things, but to lie and make it sound like I just decided to up and leave and that I was the one who had *"emotional issues"* was incomprehensible. Why couldn't he just be honest? Why was he incapable of taking any responsibility for his actions? Why was all this happening?

Once I found the girlfriend's card, hidden in his tool box, two months later, professing her love for him and how with their love anything was possible, it all became clear. He denied that it didn't start until after we were separated. In my eyes, it is the only explanation for the cruel treatment, the disengagement, treating me as if I were worthless and annoying, using "evidence" from years prior, the anger, the insistence that "we" couldn't communicate while simultaneously sabotaging any of my efforts to attempt it. It all made sense the moment I found the card. Of course, he wanted everyone to believe I had "emotional problems" and had "just packed up and moved out!" I think he needed to "awfulize" me to rationalize to himself and everyone else the terrible choice he had already made. I just wish I had known he was building a relationship with someone else sooner, so I wouldn't have felt like such a fool later. I also wish he would have told me sooner, so I wouldn't have wasted so much time hoping for something that would never happen. It felt like the ultimate rejection. We had always been able to find our way back into each other's heart, always, even after some bad situations, but I had been sensing for months that his heart was closed to me. He had been unreachable. I tried talking to him. I tried approaching him with my heart in my hand, vulnerable, longing for his eyes and his words to soften toward me. He was cold and immovable for the first time in our marriage, and at the time I couldn't understand why. I felt like I kept reaching out, and he wanted nothing to do with me. He said "we couldn't communicate," but what I saw was him sabotaging my every attempt at having a real conversation. He stonewalled. He ignored me. He was uninterested, and I was confused. Why was he saying we "just can't communicate" but not trying to actually have a conversation? For months I felt invisible as he slowly distanced himself from me. None of what he was saying made sense, and from my perception, none of it lined up with reality.

So, once he told me to leave, to move out, I was already emotionally worn down. I was confused, heartbroken, overwhelmed, and desperately seeking divine guidance. In an instant everything changed. Everything that was familiar was gone: my home, my husband, my neighbors, my whole life felt like it was crashing down around me. I didn't have a job. I didn't have any savings. I had a thousand dollars in my bank account, and I was afraid. I didn't have anything. At least that's what I thought at the time. I know now that I already had everything I needed. I had my children, a place to lay my head at night, the degrees I had worked so hard to attain, and I had my faith that God was with me in the middle of this horrible mess.

No matter how much my parents and closest friends tried to remind me of what I *did* have, it was no comfort compared to all I thought I had lost. My self-esteem was nowhere to be found. I had been discarded and already replaced within a month's time. It was like I was a worn-out tire or shoe. "Just throw it in the scrap heap, and let's find a nice, new, shiny one!"

All I could think about were his words that final day in our kitchen telling me he didn't want me anymore, and the more I replayed his words, the worse I felt. He didn't want me, and no one ever will again, I told myself. I told my parents, too. My poor parents, they were like the scaffolding holding up the shell of a person I was for several months while I tried to process what the hell just happened to my life and pull myself back together again. I lost ten pounds and started to look a little like the He-Man character, Skeletor. I didn't even realize it until I noticed how excited my dad was one day when I devoured a freshly baked bowl of bread pudding. He was so excited to see me eat he then proceeded to bring me more of it the next day or two.

"You're too thin," he finally said. "You need to eat."

I honestly hadn't even realized how much weight I had lost or that I had been forgetting to eat. I looked in the mirror, and thought,

Holy crap… I look like hell! No wonder mom keeps making the bread pudding and dad keeps pushing it to me like some drug dealer desperate to make his crack quota for the week.

My dad told me over and over, in different ways, that I was going to be okay and that this was going to end up being a positive change. I didn't believe him at the time.

"Cody, in the end, you're going to be better off. People like him don't change until they throw dirt in their face. He was never going to change. One day, you'll look back and realize this was the best thing that could have happened."

I nodded in feigned agreement, never imagining I could see this disaster as anything other than an emotional hell.

"Who's going to want me?" I asked my mom. "I'm forty years old, with three kids and soon to be divorced, not once, but *twice!* On top of that, I have no job, no savings, *nothing!* I feel like a complete loser*!*"

Then my mom would say what all good moms should in that instant.

"Cody, you are *not* a loser! You have *two* degrees. You're smart, and beautiful. You have three amazing kids. You have your family, and you have so much to offer."

"What if I'm alone *forever?*"

"You won't be alone forever. You'll find someone nice, and *normal.* You haven't even had normal for years! You probably don't even remember what that's like!"

"Well, even if I do find someone nice and normal who doesn't mind a two-time repeat divorcee with three kids who lives with her parents, I'm *never* getting married again. *Ever.* Maybe I'll just collect a bunch of stray cats and take up knitting, become the crazy cat lady of the town."

When I moved into my grandparents' old house, it hadn't been lived in for a few years, and before that, my 98-year-old grandfather had been living there alone since my grandmother passed away at the young age of 65. As you can imagine, there was a lot of dusting to be done. Right off the kitchen, there is a large, long, narrow pantry and laundry room lined with shelves on one side. We had just moved in, and I had been standing in the laundry room talking on the phone to my older sister. This house was small, and the laundry room had become the place I went to hide and talk on the phone where the kids couldn't hear me. I found a laundry basket full of clothes nestled between my grandfather's extra refrigerator and the washing machine, sat down and made myself comfortable. As I filled my sister in, she asked me if I could wait until the next school year to find a teaching job to give me some time to get myself together, to heal, and to get the kids settled.

"Do you really need to find a job *now*? I mean, a lot has just happened. Don't you think you need some time? This seems like a terrible time to have to search for a job. Maybe you could wait a year until you get the kids settled in school and get the house together and yourself together?" she asked.

"So, are you saying I'm a mess?" I replied.

Silence.

"Well, you're right. I am an emotional wreck, but I don't want to be a broke emotional wreck. I need to get a job."

"Maybe you should just slow down. You know, take some time. I can help you out if you need some money. What about your child support? Are you getting that?"

"Well, yes, but that's not enough to live on. I've got to be able to take care of myself and the kids on my own."

As much as I wished that were possible, I had to find a way to stand on my own two feet. It was July, and most schools are done hiring in the spring, so I knew my chances of finding a teaching job were likely not very good at this time of year. Plus, it had been a few years since I had even taught school. I had resigned from my previous job to stay home with our youngest daughter and to take care of my husband. The VA had started a care-giver program for the spouses of wounded vets, and my husband's case worker at the VA suggested we apply for it. We did, and we were approved for the program. My husband's injuries had been severe, and the stipend was generous. Having a baby who was frequently sick, a full-time job, two other children, and a husband who was frequently absent was a lot to handle. So, upon receiving the first stipend check and realizing we would be fine without my job, I decided to resign. Worst. Decision. Ever… Now, four years later, here I was, crying in a pile of dirty clothes in my grandparents' 1971 ranch home, jobless and husbandless, and facing the reality of job hunting.

Who is going to want to hire me? I thought. I have the confidence of a snail, the self-esteem of a slug, and a huge gap in my resume.

I hung up the phone, and for the first time an overwhelming fear welled up within me about my finances and about my future in general. Since I had been staring at the dusty shelves the whole time I was on the phone, I grabbed a rag and some cleaner and started wiping them off. As soon as I started cleaning those filthy shelves, the floodgates opened. As the tears flowed, something odd happened. The Twenty-Third Psalm welled up in my spirit, along with the tears. My mom had me memorize it when I was a child. No one was around to call me crazy for talking to myself, so I let the words come out of my mouth, along with my desperate sobs. "The Lord is my Shepherd. I shall not want," I choked out between sobs as I wiped down the shelves. I said it again, "The Lord is my Shepherd. I shall not want." I repeated it until I was no longer sobbing and afraid, but calm and at peace. As I recited those first two sentences from the Psalm aloud, I could feel the fear leaving and the peace entering my heart and mind. I said it until I believed it, and what started out as a desperate cry of fear that I would turn into some destitute woman, ended with the confidence in my spirit that if I allowed and acknowledge Him, God would shepherd me through this dark valley and into green pastures and still waters. This was my first lesson in the power of speaking Truth over my life. It's easy to become overwhelmed with emotions when you're in shock and grief, and the change I felt when I spoke Truth out loud to my situation was so powerful in that moment, I had to make it a practice. The truth was, God had my back. God would provide me with everything I needed, and by the time the last shelf was clean in that pantry, I believed it. I *believed* it.

I worked on my resume, submitted it on line to several places, and kept affirming the truth that I had a higher power looking out for me who would guide me in the right direction and take care of me. As I was growing up, my parents taught me that there was a higher power who was always with us. They gave me the gift of awareness and taught us to think beyond religion and to see the vast expanse of Spirit. They taught us that God is bigger, greater, and more loving than any one building on a Sunday. Don't get me wrong, I look forward to going to church on Sundays and any other night or day of the week, and I consider myself to be a Christian. I also know that the God who created the entire universe cannot be contained in the human minds we desperately try to squeeze him into.

My dad has always read metaphysical books. His favorite book is *Illusions,* by Richard Bach. I was in such bad shape emotionally that my dad was really trying to help me see that in the middle of difficult circumstances, the only power I had to change anything was in how I was thinking about my situation. I was praying for so many things at the time, but most of all, I was praying for my husband to want me back again. I was praying for a job and for direction. I was praying for my children and for them to be okay.

I didn't have a television set yet, so I walked over to my mom and dad's house to watch theirs. As I stepped into their house, the quiet familiarity of the home in which I grew up wrapped itself around me. I made my way into my parents' room and saw the books my dad always kept on his nightstand between two marble book ends. As I scanned the spines of the books, one in particular caught my attention. *Your Word is Your Wand, huh?* I thought. Well, reciting the 23rd Psalm aloud certainly turned my thinking around, so I figured it was worth a try. If ever in my life I needed a "magic" wand, it was at that moment. I had also watched a lady preacher on TV several years before named Joyce Meyer, and she was probably the first preacher I ever heard talk about the power of your thoughts and your speech. She modeled speaking God's Word over your life as well. I had even bought her CD series ten years prior, and listened to it several times. It had resonated with me, and I did place some scripture on note cards and tape them to my mirror. I think the difference now was, I was desperate. Back then, my life was on solid ground. Now, I was on the proverbial sinking sand, and I was looking for a hand up out of the muck. I was desperate to feel a rock beneath my feet. So I slid the book out from in between an Edgar Cayce book and a Khalil Gibran book, and sat down on the bed. I read it cover-to-cover, soaking it all in.

While the book was clearly dated, it had some very encouraging content. I had learned years before the power of speaking God's Word out loud over a situation or over myself. I just hadn't ever really done it on a consistent basis before, but desperate times call for desperate measures. I grew up in a Baptist church, and I am thankful for that because I was encouraged to study the Bible and to memorize Bible verses. I had been memorizing Bible verses since I could remember, and I began to start speaking them out loud to encourage myself out of the pit of sadness I had fallen into. I wanted out of the pit, and the sooner the better.

I took this little book home with me until the one I ordered arrived. I started taking it with me in my purse on my way to interviews. I whispered the affirmations out loud early in the morning as I sat at my kitchen table before the kids got up and tried to pray and read enough to keep myself together for my children. I was wrapping myself in scripture and positive affirmations like the bailing string holding the big round hay bales out behind the tractor barn. It was what held me together when I legitimately had every right to fall apart. Early in the morning before the kids woke up and late at night when they were all asleep, I brought my broken heart and spirit like some pitiful offering before the Lord. I brought my shame at another failed marriage, my fear that I couldn't make it on my own, and my tears over the man I still was so desperately in love with, yet who had rejected me.

I was sharing a room with my five-year-old, so after she was asleep, I would slip into the bathroom off my room, slide the old door shut, and kneel on the rug of my bathroom floor using my daughter's little footstool as my makeshift altar. I would place my Bible and my books on that plastic, orange step stool and pour out my heart to God. I was desperate, and this time in prayer was the only safe place for me to take all the hurt in my heart and let it out. I prayed the Psalms out loud every night. Once I started attending Divorce Care I would read the passages for the week during that time as well. I would repeat affirmations from *Your Word is Your Wand* like, this one:

"I let go of everything not divinely designed for me, and the perfect plan of my life now comes to pass." I started carrying the little book with me in my purse, and throughout the day when I would start to feel sorry for myself or feel afraid, I would pull that little book out and quietly declare good over my life. During my job search I would affirm,

"The divine Design of my life now comes to pass. I now fill the place that I can fill and no one else can fill. I now do the things which I can do and no one else can do."

Another one of my go-to affirmations was, "What is mine by Divine Right can never be taken from me. God's perfect plan for my life now comes to pass." The more I encouraged myself with the affirmations, the more I truly believed that no matter how messed up my life felt or appeared to be to anyone on the outside looking in, the more I believed that God really and truly did have a perfect plan for my life and for my children's lives.

Once I discovered how powerful just speaking truth over my life was, I dove into it every moment I could. I was getting stronger spiritually and emotionally. I also discovered Louise Hay and her positive affirmations, which I listened to in my car to and from work. I quietly kept trudging through the pain, one day at a time, believing the words I was speaking over myself were true. I learned to hold onto the truth in the dark moments. I learned to train my thoughts like you would train an unruly puppy. These affirmations taught me to discipline my thinking and keep my thoughts in line when they wanted nothing more than to make a bee-line for the nearest pity party. Basically, as my grandma would have said, I learned that I needed to, "watch my mouth," not only in what I said to others but in how I was speaking to myself.

RELATIONSHIPPING

Relationshipping…

No, it's not really a word. I made it up yesterday. Here's an example of its proper usage. Please use your context clues.

"While the forty-something-year-old woman was adept at relation-shipping, she loathed the prospect of dating again after years of being married."

I like the term relation-shipping better than "dating" because it's more specific than "dating." You see, dating, I have decided, is way different than relationshipping. Dating is the honeymoon period prior to the actual relationshipping, especially if you are my age and already have three children.

Dating is much less complicated than relationshipping. Dating is where he picks you up at the door at 7 pm, and you go out to a lovely dinner and a cocktail and are back home by midnight saying goodbye at your door again. Dating is like a Polaroid picture. It's an isolated time frame in a controlled environment.

Actually, maybe it's more like a selfie … a photo-shopped selfie …You know, your most flattering angles, and you're only going to show off your "good side." I mean, who answers the, "So, tell me about yourself" first-date questions with a detailed description of your most annoying personal flaws? *No one.* We're all putting our best foot forward. In dating, you're getting to know someone, and that someone is the very best version of themselves. I think I'm really good at dating. Most of us are. It's easy to have an intelligent, witty conversation when there are no distractions around, especially if you're used to being a multi-tasking teacher and mom ninja in your everyday real life. When your brain is geared up to juggle multiple little-people schedules, your own personal schedule and show up and be "on" to teach a lesson to more than a hundred students five times a day, five days a week, sitting one-on-one and talking is a piece of cake. On a date, for example, you can most likely actually focus all of your attention on the person sitting across the table from you. Newsflash … This is *not* reality!

Reality is you, in the kitchen after a ten-hour work day, stirring spaghetti sauce with one hand and texting your teenager with the other to verify pick-up time for her after school choir rehearsal. All the while this is occurring, your five-year-old is whining like Stewey on family guy over and over and over, "Mommy, mommy, mommy! I'm hungry! Mommy!" Which you know may be followed by a complete meltdown if you can't pull dinner together soon. You then realize you're out of butter and milk before also realizing you only have ten minutes to wrap this cooking thing up before it's time to pick the *other* teenager up from cross-country track practice. There's a laundry basket full of unfolded clothes on the couch, a cat on the window ledge outside staring at you and meowing incessantly because everyone forgot to feed her, toys all over the living room, and you're yelling something like, "Calgon, take me away!" That, my friend, is *real life. Now* who wants to date me? You feel me, people? Who wants to jump into *this* scene? My life is complicated. I'm busy. It's hectic. I get *tired*. I come home some days after work and don't feel like cooking, and we eat a frozen pizza. I teach *seventh graders* … let that sink in for a second. Teachers joke about there being nothing else quite like being, "teacher-tired," but it's true. Teaching can be emotionally and mentally exhausting at times, and you have to be "on" even if you're having a bad day. No matter what is going on in your personal life, you have to come and put your game face on. You can't shut your office door or hide quietly in your cubicle. You don't have that luxury. So, add in the complication of twice-divorced, three kids, and teacher-tired, and I do worry sometimes that *no one* is going to want to stick around for the long haul. These are the moments when I think maybe I'll just be single for another ten years until my kids are grown up. It's a whole different ballgame dating at 40 with three kids than it is dating in your 20's or 30's with no children in the picture. I mean what if "hot-date-guy" were to see you in the middle of *that* scene? Would he still be interested in sticking around, or would reality be too much for him? Is he just interested in dating, or is he looking for something *real*? These are the questions I have.

So many questions.

So few people with any solid advice based on real-life experience.

So many opinions.

I've noticed a pattern when it comes to people trying to give me advice on dating post-divorce. The advice I've gotten typically goes one of two ways and is always given by married people since *most everyone* I know is still married. Here they are.

1. "Just have *fun*! *Why* in the world would you want to get *serious* with anyone? Enjoy being single!"

2. "You need to be *alone* ... like for *a while*."

As you can see, this advice, while well meaning, is both contradictory and annoying! However, if you have given me this advice, just know I knew it was coming from a genuine, well-meaning place. I really do know that. However, let's start with the, "You need to be alone" advice, shall we? Let's just break it down. Here's what I say in my head when someone tells me I just need to be alone. "Helllooo? Are you *kidding* me? When was the last time *you* were alone? 1998? Like in the eighth grade for a month between boyfriends?" I nod and smile when I'm told this, but on the inside all I can think is how nice and easy it is when you're in the comfortably married and settled shoes to suggest that someone just stay single and alone indefinitely. During the week I'm so busy I can't see straight between work and kids, but every other weekend when the kids are gone with their dad, being alone is not all that great. I'm an introvert by nature, so I do enjoy my space and some alone time, but home alone watching a marathon of every Diane Lane movie I can find, including "Under the Tuscan Sun," and "Must Love Dogs" while eating a frozen dinner and drinking half a bottle of pinot noir is a little bit, well, *pathetic*.

I'm not saying I want to get married. That may never happen again, but I would like to find a companion and friend to enjoy life with. Plus, here's the thing; I *have* already been alone for a while ... like a *long* while. I mean even though I was married, the last year my husband was literally in another country for four months and totally checked out the other eight. I got really used to being alone. I got dumped by my husband in June of 2016, and it's well far into 2018, so I think that qualifies as enough alone time. The real reason I think "maybe you just need to be alone for a while" gets under my skin is this; my ex-husband is getting married tomorrow... *tomorrow*...fifteen months after our divorce was final. Why is it *I* need to be alone when my ex is getting *married*? Did anyone tell *him* maybe *he* just needed to be alone? I really do understand that what people mean is you need to fix yourself first, and I have definitely gone above and beyond when it comes to seeking out learning the lessons I needed to learn from my failed relationships. I've focused on healing. I've developed my own interests and hobbies, and most importantly, I've pursued strengthening my relationship with God. I've learned to never give my power away to a man or put him in a position in my heart and life that only God should hold. Now, I would really like someone to move forward with -- a friend, a companion, a partner. While alone isn't a bad word, it's not what I want for my present or my future. Would I rather be alone than with the wrong person? Heck yes! I would choose alone any day of the week over settling for the wrong person.

The "just have fun" advice I thought was pretty good at first, but there's a problem with it. I'm really not the type of girl who wants to just go out and have, "fun." Don't get me wrong, of course I like to have fun. Fun for me is going to hear live music, going out to eat at restaurants, going to see the latest movie, going dancing, or going to a play or a museum. Fun is great, but I also want something *real*. Better yet, I want something fun *and* real. I have dated two men in particular, briefly, who were a lot of fun. They took me to plays, concerts, and high-end restaurants. One of them I traveled with, which I also enjoy, but neither of these men was interested in building anything *real* with me. Neither of these men wanted what I want -- an actual relationship where you share your thoughts, dreams, hopes, feelings, and see a future together for your relationship. One of these men after about six weekends of "fun" dating was content talking to me a total of about five minutes a week as he traveled and worked out of town. When I questioned him about this, he said that he just really didn't like talking on the phone. How convenient! He was just interested in having "fun," so we stopped dating because in the end I want someone who *can't wait* to talk to me at the end of every day. I sure as heck was not going to waste one more minute begging someone to want to *talk* to me. No thanks!

Yes, dating is its own special adventure. It's not reality. You don't know each other yet, not really. You don't know that when I'm in a rush I have a habit of inadvertently leaving cabinet doors half open. You don't know that if we need to be on the road at 5:30 you need to lie and tell me 5:15 because it's always going to take me about 15 minutes longer to get ready to go out than I think it will. You don't know all the little things about me that you may eventually find annoying but that I really hope you'll find quirky and slightly adorable in their eventual annoyance. These are the little things you know about someone you are in a long-term relationship with, things no one else knows. You also don't know all the amazing little things about me that make me great (I hope). You don't know that I have killer dance moves in the kitchen when the kids and I break it down during a random dance-off or that I am an excellent bed-time story teller. You don't know what a hard worker I am or the hours I pull between my 4:30 a.m. wake up and my 11:00 p.m. bed time. There is so much a stranger sitting across from a table in a restaurant from you meeting you for the first, second or third date just can't know about you, and this is what I hate about dating. It's the starting over from the beginning. *Explaining* yourself. Talking about yourself, your childhood, your education, your family, your job, your work history, your exes, your marriages, your divorces, your kids, and on and on and on. God, it's *exhausting*. This is exactly why I never planned on getting divorced a second time. This is why I wanted to do anything possible to salvage my marriage. It's the little intimate details you come to know about someone that to me make relationshipping far superior to dating just for fun.

The truth is, no one is perfect. The truth is, no matter how "hot" and interesting the guy or girl is you're so excited about now on these first few dates, the shine will eventually wear off. Let's be realistic. It always does. So, it doesn't matter how this person appears at the beginning, what is going to matter in the end is are you still going to like this person one year, five years, ten or twenty years from now? How do you figure this out?

Time and observation.

Watch.

Wait.

Listen.

Learn.

This is the frustrating part of being at this stage of life and being single. I want someone beside me at the choir concerts, soccer games, track meets, and awards ceremonies. I want someone to plan a family vacation with. I want someone sitting next to me at church on Sundays and someone sitting next to me at the holidays. I look around and see families everywhere, and I realize that I *am alone*. I am beginning to get used to it, but it does make me sad. This is why I have to remind myself to be patient when it comes to dating and finding a companion. I have finally come to the point of giving up, which I see as a good thing actually. I have pretty much decided that I just don't really want to seek out someone to date.

The way I see it now is that if God wants to bring me someone to share my life with, well, He is going to bring me someone to share my life with. I'm done looking. All I do is make a mess of things when I try to be in control of anything. He is going to have to hit me over the head with a holy relationship hammer and a flashing neon sign with an arrow pointing at this man. I mean, I just can't bear to keep up the old dating "pitch." I'm done pitching myself like I'm some saleswoman desperate to close a deal. I'm *not* desperate, and I *can't* deal! I'm not cynical. I'm just ... so ... tired. If someone is going to fall in love with me, they're going to have to fall in love with the *real* me, not some sales-pitch version of me. I'm not perfect, but I think I'm pretty damn good, and I feel certain that one day, God is going to plop a person right in front of me who is equally imperfect but pretty damn good too. I'm also certain that the next love will be my last, and I'm counting on the hope that God saw way, way ahead of me and fixed it ahead of time to save the best for last. This won't be like a young love because let's face it, we're not young and that's becoming truer with every passing day. The next love will be different, and I think it's going to take my breath away. God's just like that -- full of surprises and redemption and such great grace that I am trusting He knows exactly who and what I need. So, like the great Carrie Underwood sings, "Jesus, take the wheel!" I surrender. This is hands-free relationshipping.

RUN FOR YOUR LIFE

"So what? I'm still a rock star. I've got my rock moves, and I don't need you."

—Pink

"Run for Your Life!" That's exactly what I wish I would have done the day I met my ex-husband. Since I was too dumb to do that, I'm running for it now, literally running. It's a Saturday morning in October in central Texas. I'm at my parents' ranch, and I'm just sad. It's been about a month since I discovered my husband has started a relationship with someone else and has a girlfriend. My husband has a *girlfriend*, and I am trying to find a place to begin wrapping my head around that fact. I am trying to begin to get over him, and he has already moved on to another relationship. Knowing he doesn't want to be married to me anymore is crushing, but discovering he already has someone else is both infuriating and humiliating. It feels like more grief than I can bear.

I feel more alone than ever. I feel like the tears are always there, so close to the surface that just a word could make them spill over the rim of my defiant eyelids fighting so desperately to hold them back. I feel like never getting out of bed again, but I know that isn't an option. So, I press past what I feel and do what I've been forcing myself to do until it has become a habit I've started to find solace in. It's my new best friend. When I feel like staying under the covers and hiding away from the world, I look at my shoes. I set them out the night before at bedtime where I can see them. I also set my running clothes alongside them so there's no excuse. I know if I don't gather everything together for the early morning, I might be tempted to give up when I can only find one sock at 7 a.m. on a Saturday morning. "Well, forget it, I can't run with one sock," is a true-story conversation I've had with myself. "Well, my sports bra is M.I.A., and I definitely can't take the girls out without that critical piece of gear," is also a conversation I've had with myself just before crawling back under the covers.

I'm learning to prepare so I have no excuses. I can't afford to make excuses. I have a heart to fix, and this time it's mine. I've spent the last seven years thinking and praying for my husband's heart, and maybe that was a big part of the problem. I forgot about my heart, and somehow, when I run, I feel like I'm running back to myself. More importantly, when I run, I feel like I'm running back to Source, to God. The God I had been neglecting to build a relationship with to the extent that

I once had. The one I took off the metaphorical throne of my heart and replaced with a fallible, flawed, undeserving man.

I run, and I think. I think about my Sunday-school teacher, Mrs. Wagner. I remember sitting in Sunday school wondering what in the world she was doing with a clothing iron, a strainer, a trophy and some other small objects. I can still see her clearly -- her short, brown hair, flowered cotton dress, and hear her melodic voice as she took the iron, pressed it across the table like she was ironing a shirt and said, "Not that I have already obtained all this or have already arrived at my goal, but I press on to take hold of that for which Christ Jesus took hold of me. Brothers and sisters, I do not consider myself to have taken hold of it. But one thing I do: (cue Mrs. Wagner picking up the iron again) Forgetting what is behind and straining toward what is ahead, I press on toward the goal to win the prize for which God has called me heavenward in Christ Jesus."

I trudge along the quiet road, paved loosely with caliche. If you're not from Texas, that's a dusty, white rock. There are no cars. There are no noises at all except the wind, the birds, and the sound of my tennis shoes crunching the caliche as my dirt path comes to an end and I'm forced back onto the rocks. I started running again last month, and it's helped to keep me sane. I get into a zone, and when I'm done, I always feel better that when I took the first step. I call it pavement therapy. Sometimes I cry when I run. I live in the country, and here in central Texas, where I'm running today at my parents' other cattle ranch, there is about a zero percent chance of anyone driving by and labeling me a freak for crying. Plus, I figure I could save face if needed by faking a twisted ankle in the event someone did see me.

My best friend Jenny had just mentioned to me that I should start running again because she remembered how much it helped me through my first divorce. I've always enjoyed working out, but something about running has a way of keeping me sane and centered. It's meditative to me -- the time alone, listening to music, enjoying the scenery, feeling the heat or the cold or the wind and rain, seeing the lightning bugs sparkle as the first shadow of the evening darkens the woods next to my running trail. I love all of it.

I was at the lowest point in my life emotionally when another friend of mine, Chelsea, made a Facebook post about a local charity run she had signed up for but wasn't going to able to attend. She had already paid for the run, and she was asking if anyone wanted to take her packet and racing bib and run in her place. Jenny had just encouraged me to start the running up again, and I had been thinking about it already. As soon as I saw her post, I contacted her, and she was kind enough to bring the packet by my parents' house next door while I was at work. The next morning, I woke up at 6:00 a.m. and made it to the downtown square where I live. I was alone, and I felt every ounce of the greater loneliness of feeling abandoned and betrayed as I made my way to the park in the center of downtown. I remember looking around the park, thinking maybe I would see someone I knew. This was where I had grown up, after all, but things change, places grow, and eventually with enough growth you can look around your hometown one day and not see one familiar face in the crowd.

So, there I was, awkwardly stretching, feeling out of place and unsure of myself. For so long, I had been my husband's sidekick. Wherever he went, I went too, and being out in public without him felt like walking out of the door to go to work and suddenly realizing you forgot to put your pants on. This feeling was becoming familiar to me, and I would frequently find myself having to choke back tears. I found a table and then a bench and sat around until it was time for the race to start. When it was time for the 5k, I squeezed into the crowd of runners, plugged my ear buds into my iPod, cranked up Pink's "Greatest Hits ... So Far" album, and ran. It had been a while, but it felt good. It felt great.

Pink's greatest hits album is always what I listen to when I race. I told you about the meditative part that I like about running, the calming part, but Pink's album is a perfect metaphor for the other part I love about running. It's the part where I can run out all the rage I've had to cover up with a smile. I don't have to fake it out here on the pavement. It's taking the dark energy of the anger and grief I feel and repurposing it. It's turning it into light, into fire, into the passion for life I forgot still existed deep down in my soul. Running has helped me turn the anger of betrayal and loss into a new beast, not a whining, whimpering damsel in distress, but a warrior. Not a victim, but a fighter. All I know is, if Earth was invaded by aliens, Men in Black (the first movie) style, and all the men in the world suddenly vanished, I'd want Pink to lead me into battle! Clearly, she's a bad ass.

I love how at mile two and a half I can look down at my watch and see that if I want to stay under an eight-minute 5K time, I can't quit pushing. So, I focus on Pink's voice singing. "Made a wrong turn once or twice. Dug my way out, blood and fire. Bad decisions. That's all right. Welcome to my silly life. Mistreated. Misplaced. Misunderstood. Miss know it. It's all good. It didn't slow me down."

So many of Pink's lyrics are like this. The chorus? That's even better. "Pretty, pretty please, don't you ever, ever feel like you're nothing. You are perfect." I set my mind on the fact that even though my lungs are tired, and my body wants to walk, I'm not going to stop. I dig deep, and I fight for that last half mile. I see the finish line, and I dig even deeper. I press in even harder. I find the part of me that's furious and afraid, and I embrace it. It's fuel. I can see the time on the big clock at the finish line, and it makes me even more motivated. I pick up my pace and sprint as hard as I can until I step across the line. This is how I know I won't allow one man's choice to control me. This is when I remember that I have value and worth in my own right. This drive is how I know I am alive.

The course I was running went through downtown and wound through an older neighborhood. Halfway through the race, I had a realization of how disconnected I had been from everything going on in the world since my marriage came crashing down around me a few months before. I was in trauma survival mode. Day to day survival was as far out in front of myself as I could see, and everything going on in the world, including politics and the upcoming 2016 election, was barely even in my peripheral view. My husband and I had been very involved in the local political events for the past seven years. As a wounded veteran and his caregiver, we were invited to all kinds of events. I say this so you have an idea of how much a part of our lives and our marriage revolved around what was happening politically. Every day in our house, the little TV my husband had bought to place in the corner of our kitchen was on the Fox news channel. We had several TV's in the house, and most of the time two of them were usually turned on. We had frequent discussions about what was going on in the world politically, economically, socially. We paid attention.

When I moved out, I moved into a forty-year-old home. I didn't even bring a TV. My dad moved my grandfather's tiny, old set and its cabinet sitting in the garage back into the living room, but I didn't have the wherewithal to even think about signing up for cable. I had a house to get together so my kids could get back to "normal," and I was hustling like crazy to send out resumes, interview, and trying to land a job. I discovered I didn't really miss TV so much, especially the news. I really didn't miss watching the news at all. In the big scheme of things, I started to see it as just more noise, more negative noise I simply didn't want and couldn't handle at the time.

The reality of how disconnected from everything except crisis management of my own life hit me as I ran this 5k. I passed a coral-colored, brick ranch style home and noticed the campaign sign in the front yard. It said, "Pence," and I remember thinking, *Hmm, never heard of him*, as I got closer to the sign. I figured it must be some guy running for local office. As I ran closer it said, *Pence for Vice President. Holy crap! Vice President? I really need to get cable*, I thought. I realized that until I saw that sign on the 5k course, I literally had no idea who the Republican Vice-Presidential candidate even was. Embarrassing. I was too busy trying to save my sanity and resurrect my personal life from the dust to even care about the Presidential election. So much had changed in my life, and that stupid sign reminded me of the last political event my husband and I had attended together one week before he disappeared for good.

I found myself thinking about a lot of things when I ran, working them out in my mind. So, that first race I realized I was almost to the finish line and had a lot left in my tank. I sprinted as fast and as hard as I could. Out of breath and sweating, I made my way to the side of the finish line and found a place to sit on the edge of a concrete wall. When the results came in, I was shocked to see I was fourth in my age group and just one place away from getting a medal. In that moment, watching the winners go forward to receive their medals and knowing I was so close, something magical happened inside of me. I felt a familiar fire start to grow, and a passion was ignited.

I started training and found as many local 5k races as I could to sign up for. This is when the running started to change more than I bargained for. I started running after school at dusk. I had usually spent the day holding back the tears, and when I ran, I would listen to worship music, pray silently, cry, and end up with a sense of peace at the end of the three miles. You see, I live at the end of a dead-end dirt road on a cattle ranch, and that road is not busy. So I would run and pray and cry and look for God in the sunsets and the glow of the lightning bugs dancing in the woods when it was time to get home. In a time of the most intense pain of my life, I was finding solace in running. In these moments I felt connected to God and to myself again. I was finding myself again, and I felt a little bit stronger with every step.

So today, I ran the same charity race again the second year in a row. This time, I was the "top female finisher" in the "Masters" division. When they called my name, I wasn't sure what I had won.

"Masters? What does that mean?" I asked my friend.

"It's 40 and older," he said.

"Oh. So, I'm the fastest old lady out here, then?"

"Yes, you are!" he said.

Even if I am an "old lady" runner, it still felt good to win. I felt like it was a full circle moment, getting that medal. I am grateful to have crossed the finish line this morning with a heart that's no longer broken but whole, well . . . way more put together than it was a year ago, and faith that is stronger today. I can look back and know God was carrying me through the valley of despair I was trudging through last year. Last year, I thought I had lost *everything*, and honestly, I had lost a lot. A year later, I no longer feel like I lost everything. I feel like I won. I won because I started with nothing, or what I believed at the time was nothing, and I have built a whole new life. I won because I found myself again with every mile I ran, every prayer I prayed, every tear I cried.

This second year running as I listened to Pink, I listened with new ears. This year, I could listen and agree in my heart with the lyrics that I am good enough. Better yet, I'm perfect, just the way I am.

TAKE THIS CARD AND SHOVE IT

That's right. You read it right. Take this card and shove it. Johnny Paycheck said it first. Well, sort of. Johnny Paycheck sang it, but David Allan Coe wrote it. "Take This Job and Shove It." I always did like that song. "Take this job and shove it. I ain't working here no more. My woman done left and took all the reasons I was working for." I digress. Now, back to the card and sticking it where the "sun don't shine." Oh, what card am I referring to? Well, you know, the one my ex-husband's girlfriend mailed to my house along with some gifts to my daughter. "Well, what's so awful about that?" You may be asking yourself. My answer is, a lot. There is *a lot* wrong with that.

If this were some woman he had met after we were already divorced, I wouldn't feel the same. The problem is, this woman was an integral piece of my marriage ending in the worst way possible. The problem is, almost a year ago exactly, I had found another card from this same woman, only it wasn't addressed to my daughter. It was addressed to my husband.

It didn't show up in a Fed Ex box. I found it in my husband's tool box. Opening that card from this woman was the worst moment of my life. I was completely blindsided and spent the next six months reeling from it and the cold way in which I had been discarded like an empty gum wrapper.

This "gift" and this card sent to my home address were boundary violations with a sadistic twist. It wasn't as if my ex and his girlfriend hadn't seen my daughter for a long period of time and wouldn't be seeing her again. If that were the case, considering the circumstances, the right thing for my ex to do would have just been to sign the card from him alone. They also could have just waited to do it a few days later when they saw her in person, if the purpose was to give her a gift.

I know that wasn't the purpose. It wasn't the only purpose. I believe the only reason someone would be so sadistic as to send a card from the woman he had an emotional affair with and then cheated on me with while he dragged me along with, "I love you texts" at the same time he was with her, is to mess with my head and my heart. Who would do such a thing?

My answer ... a jerk. A big, fat, mean, jerk would do such a thing. I'm not going to lie. It *did* mess with me. The house that I live in is *my* safe place. It's not the place to send a card to from the woman who cheated with my husband while I sat at home oblivious to her existence.

I felt angry, and then I felt sad. I opened the package from my daughter's dad in the middle of my kitchen table for her, not expecting to find a card from this woman. To add insult to injury, I had met this other woman years ago when we visited my husband's hometown. He invited her along with other friends to go out on the town with us. That night, this woman blatantly flirted with him right in front of my face. It was *gross. She was gross.* Her friends even told her she was being awful and apologized to me for her behavior. So, finding out my husband was in a relationship with her behind my back was even more proof that she really was a predator. Now don't get me wrong, my then-husband was even more to blame in not shutting that behavior down immediately. It takes two to tango. I just can't imagine ever disrespecting another woman in that way by coming onto her husband literally *right in front of her face.* Not only that, but our *seven-week-old baby* was back at our friends' house being watched by my mom so we could have a night out together. I mean, *who acts like that,* flirting with a married man who has a newborn baby right in front of his wife? Who would do such a thing?

My answer: *An Ass-hat*! Only an *Ass-hat* would do such a thing! (Definition of Ass-hat: "One who has their head up their ass. Thus, wearing their ass as a hat.) See... an *Ass-hat.* How not to be an Ass-Hat 101 starts with this rule: Do not flirt with other people's spouses ... I mean, does this really need explaining? Can't you get your own? Okay, you've all been schooled on the basics of ass-hattery. You're welcome. Feel free to use it wherever it may be applicable, although I only wish you an ass-hat-free life of goodness and happy rainbows.

Anyway, I had a light bulb moment ... who would want to be in a relationship with a jerk like that? My answer ... *not me.* I know I'm not perfect, but I never would have pulled a low move like that. I used to think I couldn't be happy without that jerk. Not anymore. It's been a long time coming for me to be able to accept the reality that I was married to someone whose "love" really wasn't love at all. Everybody told me while I was stuck dead in my tracks, deeply grieving the loss of my marriage, that I was better off. I didn't believe them. *Better off? I would think to myself. This doesn't feel like better off, I thought. This feels like a pit of despair. This feels like the worst thing that's ever happened to me. This feels ... worse than it must feel like to be a real ass-hat! How am I better off?*

But now, I know that they were all right. I *am* better off. I *do* deserve better, and now *I know it*. When I look back at the cruelty of the "discard" phase of my relationship with my ex, I realize that the attention, idealization, and appreciation he showered on me in the beginning were also just a phase for him. None of it was real. It was only temporary until the devaluation stage of our relationship began. First, I was perfect. He bragged on me to everyone, all the time. He wanted me with him all the time. So, he married me. Then once he had me, it started very quickly to feel like he didn't want me at all. Once he married me, I figured he would act like a husband. That seemed like a completely reasonable expectation to me.

"Why did you even ask me to marry you if you don't want to be a husband?" I remember saying. I kept hoping it would go back to the way he treated me in the beginning, but that never happened. He devalued me more and more with each passing year, and if I dared react, I was labeled, "*crazy*." He could disappear for days with no communication and expect me to be completely happy, or go to a bar and stop answering his phone and not show up until the next morning, and if I reacted, I was just, "*crazy.*" He would tell family and friends a fraction of the truth, which was my reaction to his bad behavior, but never the truth about what he was doing and saying to me. It was as if all those people he bragged to about me, he now wanted to convince that I was unstable, awful, and "*crazy.*" I know I was having normal reactions to an extremely abnormal situation and doing the best I could to survive. The only thing I did that was truly, "crazy," was to *stay and accept how badly I was treated.*

Acceptance. The word can bring healing or pain. Accepting repeated bad behavior and accepting being treated cruelly invites pain. For months I did not, could not bring myself to accept that my marriage was over. I prayed that my husband would wake up and realize he had made a terrible mistake choosing this other woman over me. What did she have that I didn't? I could not understand it. That never happened. He moved her into our house, and he signed the divorce papers three weeks later.

People tell you that it will just take time to feel better after a breakup. They repeat the cliché that "time heals all wounds." I think they're wrong. I don't think the time is what heals the wounds of betrayal and loss. I think accepting reality, really accepting it, is what allows you to heal.

I am so full of gratitude that I have at last reached the stage of acceptance in my journey of grief. The trip from shock and disbelief, to denial, then to anger, then to depression, then recycling those stages for months was the worst trip of my life, but I think I have finally arrived at the doorstep to acceptance. I'm finding there are many layers of acceptance when the loss is complex. That's okay. I'm just so thankful I am finally here. The more I accept my new reality, the more peace I am finding, and that's really the ultimate goal now.

So, as my daughter looked at what her dad and his girl-friend sent, I held my tongue and plastered on a big, fake smile. As she smiled, I smiled back and agreed with feigned enthusiasm that the stuffed animal was indeed, "so cute!" On the inside, my heart felt like it was in my throat. I was shocked to see the card, but I wasn't going to allow my hurt to hurt my daughter. I suggested she take the box to her toy closet and find a place for it there, and she happily ran away. I knew this wouldn't be the last time I had to fake a smile and hide my feelings, and I also knew I didn't have a choice.

While I will never accept this other woman as someone I think is of a worthy character to be a part of my daughter's life, I will never make my daughter feel bad or guilty about loving her own father or his questionable choice of compan-ions. I will choose to keep that to myself. My daughter has every right to love her father. That isn't my place, and what he does and who he does it with is no longer my concern so long as my daughter is safe, cared for, and looked after when she is with him. My job is to shield her from the truth, and I can accept that because I love her more than I loathe the choices of my ex.

Plus, let's not forget the universal law that what you put out into the universe is going to come back around to you like a boomerang and smack you right upside your head. "Ka-POW!"... It just is. There really isn't a way around it. So, at least there's that. Vengeance need not be mine. I'll leave that up to Karma, the gift that truly keeps on giving.

YOU THINK YOU KNOW
SOMEONE

Recently, I got a call from my cousin Laura, whom I adore, telling me that her husband had run off with a woman he worked with. The thought of her standing with her girls in the driveway, tears running down all their faces as they begged him not to go. made me want to hunt the man down and go Carrie Underwood, "Maybe Next Time He'll Think Before He Cheats" on him. Instead, I decided to write this for her because I know exactly how it feels when you think you know someone one minute, and the next you don't even know where they live.

You think you know someone. You fall in love. They're crazy about you. You're crazy about them. Everything is perfect. They ask you to marry them, and you say yes. Flash forward sixteen years. You have two young daughters, a home, and those two things have been your job, your responsibility for the past twelve years since your oldest daughter was born. You are well educated. You have a degree in business, and before

105

you had babies, you had a good job. You chose to stay home and raise your girls, take care of your home, support your husband -- you know, the one you're still crazy about. This is your life. Your husband, your home, and your children are literally your life purpose. You have invested all your time, energy, and youth into your family. You fully expected the investment would pay off. You imagined yourself and your husband in your '60s, retired, traveling, spending holidays in familial bliss with your successful children and their children all together.

The only problem is, he's not crazy about you anymore. Even worse, you've found out he's crazy about someone else, and this someone else happens to be someone younger he works with. While you have invested your time in what many would agree is the most important job in the world -- raising your kids -- your husband has climbed the corporate ladder. He just made CEO. He's kind of a "big deal." You just made a chicken casserole, a batch of homemade cookies, and several trips back and forth between two different schools for extra-curricular activities. You haven't had a raise, ever. You haven't won any awards or received much recognition at all except for the smiles, hugs, and occasional thank-you's from your daughters. You didn't do any of this begrudgingly, you did it out of love. You thought you and your husband were a team. Now, he's left your team for a new one, and you feel lost.

You try to talk to him, but he refuses to communicate. You ask yourself what you did wrong. You ask yourself, "What's wrong with me?" If you are in this situation currently, have

been in this situation, or know someone who is, this is important, so listen. There is *nothing wrong with you -- nothing.* There
is something wrong with *him.* There is also something wrong
with any woman who would chase after a man they know damn
well is married to a good woman with two daughters at home.
So, let me add to what I said. There is something very wrong
with *her,* the other woman, and there is something very wrong
with *them* -- not you. Period. If you need to go on-line to
Amazon right this second and search for your own "Bullshit"
button to remind yourself of this fact, do it now! Stop asking
yourself, your mom, your best friend, your counselor, your
pastor, your cat, your dog and your kid's parakeet, "What's
wrong with me that he would leave me for another woman?"
I've just given you the answer. Nothing.

So, now what? Now what the hell are you supposed to do?
You cry all the time when your kids aren't looking, you cry
yourself to sleep, you cry in the middle of the night, you cry
in the morning when you are half asleep, hoping this is all just
a very, very bad dream. Your heart is in your stomach. You can
barely breathe. You only go on because your kids need you.
You are an emotional wreck, but no one would know from
the smile you've learned to fake. I know, though, and every
woman who is and has been in your shoes knows exactly how
you feel, and we want you to remember that the fact, the *fact*
that your lying, cheating, low-life scum of a husband doesn't
see your value, does not mean you are worthless. You are a
gem. You are a rock. You are the hero your girls are going to

look up to for the rest of their lives because of how strong you are going to become through all of this.

I know you still love your husband, but you have to let him go now. Nothing you say is going to change his mind. Nothing. He has made up his delusional mind that he wants this skanktrulescent ho. He *thinks* he is happier without you. Let him think what he wants. Let him be lost. Let his sorry ass go. I know your heart is broken. I know you can't see your future without him right now, but guess what? There *is a future without him,* and that future is going to be wonderful. It's going to hurt for a while. It is. It's going to hurt like hell, but one day it won't hurt like it used to. It won't hurt like it does right now. I promise you.

I thought my life was over. There were moments where I wanted it to be over, but I knew I couldn't do that to my children or my family. I know there are moments the betrayal and how he treats you as if you are an insignificant stranger after all these years is so painful, you literally feel like dying. So, listen to me. Your life is not over. With every ending, there has to be a new beginning. It's the law of the Universe.

It feels like the end of the world right now but remember that endings make way for new beginnings. This is a beginning in disguise. I was reminded of this just yesterday as I was readingWayne Dyer's book, *Change Your Thoughts, Change Your Life*. In a chapter titled, "Living with Constancy," he writes, "The reality is that beginnings are often disguised as painful endings. So when you know that there's a constant beyond the present moment's disappointment, you can sense that 'this too shall pass;' it always has and always will. When you change the way you look at things, the things you look at change!"

Your life has revolved around your husband. Not anymore. Now is the time you begin to find yourself again, and you will. You will rediscover the core of who you are, examine your values, strip down past the surface level of niceties to the essence of your spirit. You will uncover talents and abilities buried within you, lying dormant while you were so busy worrying about where your husband was and grieving the slow death of a love you were never willing to give up on. You will find out just how strong you are, and in spite of the pain you are feeling now, you are going to come out of this valley with life lessons learned and a wisdom that can only come about through trials. So dig in. Find a quiet spot and listen to your heart. It's beating. Take a deep breath. You're still here. Close your eyes and whisper a prayer, "God, I trust you. Show me who you are. Remind me who I am. Make a way for me where there is no way." He is there as close as the air you breathe and the heartbeat in your chest. Remember this when you start to feel alone. Remember that you are not alone. You never have been, and you never will be. You are loved. You are whole. You are perfect, and though you may not feel that or see that now, it's true. Just hold on.

I know you are hurting, so I don't ask you to believe me yet. I do ask that you remind yourself, on the bad days, that your feelings are temporary. This too shall pass. This winter of sorrow will come to an end, and the spring time of renewal will come. You will look up one day and see just a tiny green bud appearing from the gray, barren branches, and you will be amazed. So, prepare to be amazed! Better days are ahead of you.

BACK IN THE SADDLE AGAIN

Love is like a virus. It can happen to anybody at any time.

Maya Angelou

I never thought I would find myself anxiously awaiting a call or, in these times a text, from a man again, but here I am checking my phone to make sure it's still in working order. My divorce is final, I've worked on myself, and it's time to get back out there, whatever that means. I feel like I'm in high school all over again. Back then, circa 1991-1994, my big sister Stacey had a powder blue, light-up, push-button telephone. Our house was old school. It only had one phone outlet back in our little wing of the house, and that so happened to be in my sister's room right next to mine. Lucky for me, it had an extra-long cord I was able to stretch across her room and slide underneath my bedroom door for a little bit of privacy. Looking back now, things were so much simpler. If a boy liked you, he would call you. There was no social media, no smart phones, no Snapchat, no dating apps, no Internet! Ah, those were the good old days. While so much has changed, one thing feels very familiar: the waiting. Do you remember the excitement and anxiety of waiting on your crush to call? Do you remember the disappointment when he didn't? I'd like to say dating at forty isn't so much different from what it was at fourteen, but that would be a lie. This is *way* worse.

Sorry, I don't mean to scare you, but it's a little intimidating out here if you haven't jumped back into the dating world yet. Just brace yourselves before you jump in. On second thought, do more than brace yourselves. You may need to train for this -- like, warrior mindset training. Maybe I should say, steel yourself. Steel yourself as in, take a heart-sized steel cage, wrap that sucker around your heart, mind, emotions, and especially your vagina, and put that key away for safe keeping until some lucky individual has *proven* through *consistent actions* that he or she is worthy of gaining access to any of your aforementioned precious possessions.

I'm totally serious. Don't unnecessarily put yourself out there for any more potential disappointment and rejection before you have gotten yourself together. There's no rush. Trust me. My best advice would be to wait. Don't start dating until you have your head together again, especially if you experienced a great deal of rejection and betrayal with the ending of your marriage. You need to have worked through all of it. I thought I had worked through those things to a great extent, with counseling and a divorce support group, and addressing the spiritual side of healing, but fears related to trust have risen up in me now that I'm trying to date. So take some time to rebuild yourself, invest in your interests and hobbies, and basically just have a life of your own before you start putting yourself out there for someone else's "approval." I've made a list of some of the new and improved challenges of dating in the world of technology. Enjoy!

THE NEW CHALLENGES OF DATING AS A 40-SOMETHING

1. Texting. What is this, the stone ages? I mean, come on. I should just hand you a torch and a rock to scrape some hieroglyphic symbols on your man cave. News flash boys -- there's this crazy old-fashioned idea we refer to as calling someone. You guys have big thumbs anyway. It has to be hard to hit the right letter with those big, manly, meaty thumbs! So, why not save yourself the trouble and just *talk* to us. Yes, talk to us. Oh, is that too scary? Then guess what, I don't want to date you! Because if you can't handle having a conversation on the phone at the beginning of a relationship, then I'm definitely worried about your communication abilities over the long term. Oh, you're too busy to call me now? Dude, we've been dating for six weeks; if you're too busy now, when all of this is new and exciting, do I really think you're going to have time to call me if we make it to two years from now?

No, thank you. Now, this is just my opinion. I know people feel differently about this, and I know there are exceptions, say the true introvert who just isn't quick on his or her feet when you add in the nerves of dating. That, I get. That should also be pretty obvious to you after a first or second date whether or not he or she is just a little shy.

However, if your date is Mr. Personality in person, talking to the waiter, the hostess, the strangers at the next table, with no awkward silences where you have to carry the conversation, and then he goes radio silent during the week, I think that's a little odd. Bottom line: call us. Maybe text asking, "Hey! Thinking about you and would love to hear your voice. When would be a good time to call?" Obviously, this is post first date. I'm just saying, I would appreciate such a text. I think texting is a good way to touch base and let each other know you're thinking about them, but don't forget the value of actually giving a girl a call.

2. Selfies. No. Nope. Not gonna do it. I'm sorry, but don't ask me to send you a selfie. I'm not 21, I don't have my duck face perfected, and I'm not interested in seeing my fine lines that close up. Trust me, neither are you.

3. Dating Apps and Hook Ups. Step away from all the swiping left and right, for the love of all that is holy! What are you doing? Why would you want to "hook up" with a *complete* stranger? Call me old-fashioned,

but this seems like an insane idea to pick someone out for a one-night stand like you're shopping for a pair of shoes on Amazon. I know I'm being judgmental right now, so forgive me if you are lighting the fires in the sheets with Tinder. I just can't relate. Plus, the first man I dated post-divorce was, unbeknown to me, an avid connoisseur of hook-up, er I mean, "dating" apps.

4. On-line dating websites. I never in a million years would have said I would sign up for an on-line dating website, like not a *million*, but I did. Here's why. If you are divorced with a busy career and children, no one needs to explain why this could be an option. When you are a single, working parent, and a good parent, you simply don't have time to be out mingling and meeting people. Plus, in the places you go to: dance lessons, soccer practice, your workplace, almost everyone is married! So, I figured out pretty quickly how difficult it is to meet quality single men with whom you are compatible. However, I found out you have to be really careful. There are lots of con artists out there. I tried on-line dating for a very short time, but in the end decided I would rather trust that the person I was supposed to be with would make his way into my orbit.

There are some things I did like about on-line dating sites. Assuming everyone is honest on their questionnaire about who they are, these sites are supposed to match you with individuals who are compatible with you. Along with pictures, you get information about what is important to them, what their hobbies are, who has been the biggest influence in their lives, what are things they couldn't live without if they had to list five, and how they say the people who know them the best would describe them. Again, assuming they are honest, these profiles help narrow down people you might have an interest in meeting. The problem, of course, is that people lie. Surprise! While it's no guarantee, I also feel that meeting someone on a match-making website, you are more likely to weed out the people who are just looking for a hook-up. This is just my personal opinion. I will back this opinion up with the dates I have had through on-line dating. The four or five I have been on, we met for either lunch or dinner at restaurants, and the men were very polite, respectful, and it was clear they were looking for a companion and a connec-tion, not a hook-up. I met some nice men, but after meeting them in person, there was only one I really clicked with who at the end of the first date asked for a second date. So, while everyone may not have this same experience, for me at least, I didn't meet any creeps. One guy did ask me if he could touch my hair, but that was as weird as it got. Yes, a man seriously asked me if he could touch my hair. Don't worry. I said no! I should also say that I am extremely picky, and that out of over fifty messages I received on the website from interested men, I only responded to five. So, be picky.

Basically, it's kind of a jungle out there. At this stage I'm looking for someone with whom I can enjoy life and who will be a supportive companion. I want someone who is trustworthy, honest, and loyal. Okay, maybe I'm looking for a dog and need to pay a local visit to the animal shelter, or maybe I'll keep hoping there is someone out there who isn't perfect but is perfect for me.

The last advice I'll give about on-line dating comes from a family member of mine, my Uncle Jonathon, who is a therapist. He was really sweet to check up on me after my divorce and we met for coffee a few times to discuss things when I started dating. What he told me was that research pretty much shows most men on dating web sites are just looking to hook-up while most women are looking for a relationship. His very wise advice to weed out those wanting an actual relationship was a "ten-date" rule. His advice was to wait at least ten dates before being intimate to make sure the other person wasn't just looking for sex with no intention to commit in the long run. Obviously, someone probably isn't going to hang in there for ten dates with no action if that's all they're looking for. I think this is wise advice for dating all-around, even if you meet someone the old-fashioned way. I know there are both men and women who after a divorce just want to "have fun" with no strings attached, and I guess that works fine for some people. It just isn't for me. While I'm not looking to run off and get married, I'm also not looking to be used like some object. That seems counterproductive to gaining back your sense of self.

All I know is dating is a totally different ball game post-forty with kids, and this girl is definitely a rookie.

MAGICAL PINGS

I am in charge. I take my own power back.

—Louise Hay

I t's 6:57 p.m. on a freezing evening in January, and I've just checked my cell phone for the fifth time in an hour. There's something about the cold that makes me feel just a little more lonely than normal, and there's something about the radio silence on the other end of the communication line from my new boyfriend that is magnifying it even more. Yes, I said *boyfriend*. I haven't used this word in years, and even typing it out feels strange. He referred to me in passing conversation as his girlfriend this week, and I liked hearing that. I liked it a lot. I like *him* a lot. Which is both exciting and terrifying all at the same time.

Since my divorce, I have struggled with the feeling that my life is somehow "lacking" without a romantic relationship. I remind myself that I've needed time to learn to love myself again, to reconnect to my own soul. I remind myself that I needed time to reconnect to God, the real "anchor" for my soul. I remind myself of all these truths, but deep down, I still want to be in a loving relationship. I want love, romance, and a connection with a partner who adds joy and meaning to my life. I want to build something that lasts.

Funny, when I express these sentiments to other people, they tell me not to "rush things." They remind me that many people who are married and in relationships are not happy at all and wish they were single.

I've had people tell me that if they ever got divorced or something bad happened to their husbands that they would *never* get married again.

"Just date a lot of men!"

"Play the field!"

"Have fun!"

I've heard these comments a lot, from married people who have someone lying next to them at night. It's so easy to judge me for wanting more. Just because I've been married and divorced twice, doesn't mean I don't still want a successful romantic relationship that will last. I long for it. So, when I met this man a few months ago, I realized he was someone I could see myself with for a very long time.

He is hilarious. He's charming and witty, While I know he is "into me" while we're together, it's the in-between part that is the current problem. I feel like I am out of sight, out of mind. My heart sinks even deeper as the morning turns into late afternoon, and I still haven't heard a peep out of my long-distance boyfriend. Let's add to the pile of feeling like a lonely loser the fact that I just found out my ex-husband is getting married.

"I must be really easy to forget about," I tell myself and immediately realize I am on the edge of jumping off the cliff of sadness into a full-blown pity party.

My thoughts are beginning to spiral downward, and I know I must get a grip on them. I know that I am giving my power away to people and circumstances. I know that I alone am in charge of my thoughts, actions and attitudes. The logical reasoning portion of my brain is screaming at me, "Hello? Do you see a problem here? You are obsessing! You are a great catch. You are smart, hardworking, funny, interesting, sweet, and loving. There is *nothing* wrong with you. So, *stop it!*"

The kids are all occupied in their own rooms, so I retreat to mine to try to distract myself from stalking my own stupid cell phone. I stare at the stack of books scattered on my bedside table, grab the one on top, and get comfortable on my bed.

I think of Psalm 46:10. "Be still and know that I am God." I think of all the meanings I have ever learned about those two words: be still. I've seen it translated as, "stop fighting, be in awe, stop striving, return, let go." In context, there is a war going on. I realize there is a war going on in my mind and in my heart. I know that until I stop fighting, stop, and decide to acknowledge and become aware of God's presence and power, I am only going to make matters worse. By now, I have learned where to turn for help when my heart is not in great shape. I go where I can get still and try to listen. I open my Bible to Psalms 18:2. "The Lord is my rock, my fortress, and my deliverer, my God, my rock, in whom I take refuge, my shield and the horn of my salvation, my stronghold." As I silently read these words, I take a deep breath, reminding myself of who I am.

I set my Bible down on my bedside table and pick up the other book I have sitting nearby. I crack open Wayne Dyer's, *Change Your Thoughts, Change Your Life,* knowing my thoughts have been swirling around like the West Texas sand in a dust storm. I am aware of how my body feels in these moments when I start to fear: unsettled, tense, exhausted. My thoughts have gone astray and taken my focus with them. I turn to the chapter about letting go, going with the flow of life, and living in a way that is not resistant to change but accepting of the natural order and timing of life. The thoughts of, *How did I get here? This is not where I am supposed to be in life at my age. Things shouldn't be this way,* make their appearance more frequently these days as I'm trying to start dating again. It isn't easy, and it wasn't what I had planned. Dr. Dyer writes, "Peace is the result of retraining your mind to process life as it is, rather than as you think it should be." Accepting life as it is isn't always easy, but it's necessary for moving forward.

I hear the familiar "ping" of an incoming text, and I feel a sudden surge of hope. I snap to, throw the book I'm reading off my lap, and lunge for my phone faster than a starving man fighting for the last piece of bread. The little green rectangle pops up, and I'm hoping with all my heart to see the name, "Tom" as the heading of the text. Instead, I see, *"Mom…"* I sigh and flop myself back onto my bed. *Of course, I hear from her,* I think. *She has to love me.* The moment of hopefulness gives way to a wave of disappointment. I pick the book back up and try to focus. "Be content with what you have; rejoice in the way things are. When you realize there is nothing lacking, the whole world belongs to you." I tell myself this is true. However, I've gotten myself into my first long-distance relationship since I was twenty years old, and this time around I thought technology would make it easier. In some ways it has, but in this case, it makes any lack of communication seem inexcusable because let's face it, it's just so easy to communicate now. We not only have texting, but a million other apps created to keep you connected to loved ones. Add to this the fact that my ex-husband would drop communication for days, and I realize this whole communication aspect of dating is going to be a real bitch, I mean, er … "growth opportunity."

This is ridiculous, I think. *Why am I sitting here waiting all day for him to call or text? It's not like he has to go through the trouble of writing a note with a quill, an inkwell and a calligraphy pen, for God's sake. It's not like once the note is written he must seal it with wax and summon a freaking carrier pigeon to send it to me! He has a cell phone. How hard is it to pick it up, pound out a quick, 'Good morning! I just wanted you to know I'm thinking about you. Have a wonderful day.' Do you want to know how long that takes because I literally just timed it on my cell-phone stop watch? It took me twenty-seven seconds -- twenty-seven SECONDS! If I'm not worth twenty-seven seconds of your time, then I don't think I'm worth very much at all.*

If you relate to this in any way, my guess is, there's a part of you that wishes texting didn't even exist. It's a blessing and a curse, and the ease with which you can communicate, be it extremely ineffective in many ways, creates new problems when it comes to dating and relationships. So as much as I keep reminding myself to be content with the way things are, I'd really like to exclude the way things are when it comes to figuring out dating in the era of smart phones.

"Text me."

This was not in my dating vocabulary in 1998. It's 2018. It's been twenty years since I graduated college, and when I graduated college, I didn't have a cell phone. I had a telephone. It was cordless, but it was still attached to a land line. The biggest change to communicating in my youth was the invention of cordless phones and call-waiting. If you're not old enough to remember how bizarre it was to be able to walk around your house untethered from a cord attached to the wall, just trust me, it was mind-blowing at the time. As if that wasn't amazing enough, we were introduced to call waiting. Sounds great eh? Never miss a call again! I soon realized this newfangled call waiting was really annoying. They should have named it call *not waiting*. Now, instead of just waiting until later to call if the line was busy, you had the power to completely interrupt another conversation.

"I'm sorry, could you hold please?"

This phrase was no longer a line solely reserved for receptionists. Now, you had your best friends, boyfriends, your mom, even your grandmother, asking if you could "Please hold," while they checked to see who it was on the other line. After all, it could be someone *important*.

I'm old enough that I had an answering machine in my first apartment, and if anyone left me a message, I had to wait until I got home to listen to it. The key word here is *wait*. I think there is something to be said for the discipline of patience when it comes to dating. I find myself having very little patience lately. I have succumbed to the present-day millennial mindset of wanting things now. What is it that I really want now? It's a partner, someone I can share life with. I want someone who wants to do "real life" with me, who cares about what I think and how I feel. I want to give that kind of love, and I want to receive that kind of love.

Just yesterday, I had an honest conversation with myself about my impatience and what I think is me tottering on the edge of neediness. Impatient and needy is a bad combination, and I spent yesterday attempting to center myself and back myself away from that dangerous ledge. How did I end up here on this ledge when I have been intentional and worked hard at re-building a fulfilling life for myself? I have hobbies and interests, a job and co-workers I actually like, three wonderful children who keep me on my toes, and my writing to keep me occupied and challenged.

So, why was I losing my mind on my unplanned snow-day off yesterday because the man I am dating didn't text or call me in the morning? Why did I start imagining he was having a rendezvous with someone else when he still hadn't called at 8:00 p.m.? He had texted me, and I knew he was "slammed" at work, had hours' worth of conference calls, expense reports, and Power Points to create, yet I still felt neglected and ignored. I started asking myself questions like, "Does he really even like me? Can't he find a measly five minutes before 8:00 p.m. to call or text? Why am I suddenly the one initiating the contact between us? Is there some kind of manual to help me understand this?"

I started to spiral downward into second-guessing everything I know when I am in his presence. In his presence, I'm happy. He is attentive, affectionate, and kind. He is laid-back and funny. He is 100 percent "into me." During the week is a different story, and this is where I can feel my neediness and impatience amp up from a slow simmer to a rolling boil the longer it is that I don't hear from him at all. I notice that this isn't just a one-time occurrence. The disconnect has become a pattern, and I know all about patterns. I have so many questions, and of course I try to answer them on my own, analyzing it practically to death. Why do I feel so insulted by a lack of contact? Am I being irrational? Are my expectations too high?

I decide that I feel insulted because with the technology we have at our fingertips every moment of the day, there really doesn't seem to be a good excuse for not keeping in touch. It's so easy. It really requires very little effort to send someone a quick, "Thinking about you" text. Maybe that's why I feel so offended by the long silences. I feel like someone not putting forth even the slightest amount of effort that a quick text takes, which is basically none, is saying you don't mean very much to them at all. So, I'm back to that same familiar feeling of being the one putting forth the effort in the relationship while the man is too detached to even care.

Here's the difference. A year and a half after my ex-husband and I separated, I finally see that someone who is indifferent, disconnected emotionally, and makes me feel like the crazy one for wanting the basic foundation of any relationship, meaningful communication and an emotional connection, is not someone I really want to be with anyway. It's disappointing.

It's a shame. It's a shame because I realize that some people simply don't know how to create a deep connection. They float on the surface of the ocean, content to never dive any deeper. Floating takes little effort, and you miss the beauty of what lies underneath. Maybe this man is a floater, and maybe I am a deep-sea diver. Because I'm stubborn, part of me wants to float with him for a while simply because it's lonely out on the ocean all by yourself, and I like his company. Part of me wants to take his hand and show him what's beneath the surface, and part of me doesn't think I have the energy to teach someone else how to swim. Let's face the truth, if someone isn't willing to put forth much effort six weeks into a relationship, why would you think they would put in any more effort six years in? So, for now, it looks like it's just me and the ocean. That's okay because it's not just any ocean. It's an ocean of possibilities.

THE DATING HOKEY POKEY

I'm sitting here in my local Panera Bread restaurant trying to stay busy and not think about the fact that it looks like I will likely spend the next few days completely alone. It wouldn't be so bad except that New Year's Eve is this Sunday. It's Friday, December 29, and this morning my date canceled on me, for the second day in a row. He had booked me a plane ticket to fly to Dallas to see him yesterday, then texted me that he wasn't feeling well. He rescheduled my flight for today but texted me again this morning that he still wasn't feeling well and we would need to reschedule. Obviously, the man can't help it that he's sick. So, why am I upset?

I'm not upset about the fact that he's sick. What I'm upset about is the delivery. First of all, what is the deal with people not calling? I am truly beginning to have more of a hate/hate relationship with texting than my previous love/hate relationship. The text factor and the lack of any audibly detectable disappointment on his end have me feeling blown off. It's the "He's just not that into you," vibe, which is confusing because prior to this moment, I've seen nothing except evidence that he was *really* into me. Men are confusing. Dating is so freaking confusing! When I offered to come help take care of him, pass the Kleenex, and make him hot tea and chicken-noodle soup, his response was negative. It was clear to me that he really doesn't want me there, and he didn't seem disappointed at all. If he is disappointed, I certainly couldn't tell. So, I'm feeling more than a little sorry for myself. I of course text my girlfriends who try to reassure me that often, men can behave like big, giant babies when they're sick, and I can chalk it up to the sick factor. I want to believe this, but could he at least *fake* a little disappointment?

I'm trying to find the upside in this. Number one: being alone gives me time to write. Number two: being alone means I can go for a long run, work out, read a book, watch whatever I want, and take an undisturbed nap. I should be grateful for this time alone to reflect.

If I could sum up my experience with being single again and trying to date, the word I would use right now would be disappointing. I'm hopeful, though, that these disappointments will make it all the sweeter if I ever do meet a man who sticks.

It's freezing cold and bleak and gray outside. Granted, the man I was supposed to fly to see is sick with bronchitis, but still, booking and then canceling a flight to see him twice in two days is a very disappointing turn out for the New Year's weekend.

"I don't care," was my response to his declaration of illness. "I don't care if we sit around with a box of Kleenex eating bowls of chicken-noodle soup all weekend. I miss you and was looking forward to seeing you."

"Honestly, I feel like crap, and I really just want to be alone."

"OK. I understand," I lie. I don't understand. This really wasn't the way I saw this weekend going at all. I had bought a new dress and spread a fourth of my closet out on my bed picking outfits to pack. The kids left yesterday with their dads.

I recognize the feeling of hurt and rejection, and I know it isn't rational to feel this way. "Okay, my daughter is beeping in," he says. "I'll talk to you this afternoon."

"Don't bother," I reply. I hear the words come out of my mouth before I realize what I'm saying. "Well, that's not very productive," he retorts. He's right. It isn't. It's just mean, and I immediately realize maybe I'm not as ready as I thought I was to date. It's my baggage knocking on the door of my heart again, and unfortunately, I just let it come waltzing right in.

I hang up the phone and wonder what in the hell is wrong with me? I can't even tell anymore if my reaction is reasonable or not. I feel like two back-to-back relationship betrayals have left me warped, not trusting my own intuition, and suspicious. What I don't want to become is cynical. There are so many things about trying to date at this age and season of my life that I just don't know. I do know one thing ... lately, I've felt like I'm sitting around waiting for him to call and then chronically disappointed when after waiting 24 hours to hear his voice he is ready to hang up in less than ten minutes. I just don't get it. He seems really into me when we're together.

He says he would even be willing to move here where I live if things keep going well between us, and yet it seems like he has zero desire to actually talk to me or ask about my day or what I've been up to or what I think. As a matter of fact, not only has he said he would move here to see if we could work it out, we went to look at homes together. I don't want to be with someone who is not willing or capable of connecting on an emotional level. I am not a business transaction. I am a woman, and I need connection.

I've noticed a pattern that this man really does not like to talk on the phone. He keeps the interaction very short and surface level, which wouldn't be a problem except we live about three hours from one another. "Why am I feeling rejected?" I question myself. "The poor man is sick!" He certainly sounds sick. I know it is a legitimate reason to cancel my flight twice, but because I'm a hopeless romantic at heart, that's not what I want to hear. I guess what I want to hear is, "I feel like crap, but I miss you. So, if you're okay with knowing it's going to be a weekend full of hot tea, Netflix, and naps, please come see me." That's what I want. I'm hoping there's a cure for the hopeless romantic part of me. That part is very unrealistic and impossibly ideal. Maybe the cure for it is to keep dating because frankly, it sucks. Sooner or later, the hopeless romantic will likely throw in the towel and settle for just a dab of romance. Maybe accepting reality will lead to contentment and realistic expectations.

They say the person in the relationship who "cares the least," holds the most power in the relationship. Think on that one. I am right in the middle of experiencing this theory, and I have to say, I think that's true, seeing as I suddenly feel so vulnerable and thrown off my game. What do I mean by "my game?" I mean I have come to a place where I am at peace, moving to my own rhythm. There is a part of me that relishes the quiet stillness of my home on the Saturday and Sunday mornings when I am by myself. I have a routine. I make my coffee, I sit at the kitchen table in the same spot. I read, I surf my social-media account with no one looking over my shoulder to judge the amount of time I'm wasting. I can write and think. I take my time. I take care of myself, and a part of me cherishes the alone time. I've gained confidence and was actually feeling like I had my self-esteem back. So why is this glitch making me want to freak out? I'm doing my best not to spiral into a pre-New Year's Eve depression, but it's making me wonder if I will have the ability to maintain this balance I've created when I add another person into the equation.

Now, my life doesn't revolve around a man, and I don't ever want to slip up and go back to living that way again. I have tried to center my life around God, my kids, my work, and my family. I've re-discovered my gifts and talents. I'm playing guitar and writing songs again. I'm getting involved in church. I've planned trips and traveled on my own. I'm investing in myself again. My fear now is that I won't be able to maintain this power if I fall head-over-heels in love with someone again. This fear makes me want to hold back.

I know that in the beginning, it's smart to hold back, guard your heart, play your cards close, and take the time to observe exactly how this other person thinks and behaves. However, at some point, don't you just have to take a leap of faith and decide to dive right in with your whole heart? You know, like the love Hokey Pokey.

If you've never done the Hokey Pokey, boy you have missed out. If you've never done the Hokey Pokey on roller skates, you must take yourself immediately to the nearest roller rink and fix that. The Hokey Pokey has you throwing your appendages in and out, shaking them, and then has you turn yourself around before you clap along with the affirmation, "That's what it's all about!" For example, "You put your right arm in. You put your right arm out. You put your right arm in, and you shake it all about. You do the Hokey Pokey, and you turn yourself around. That's what it's all about."

It's great fun, apparently, when you're like five years old. It's not so much fun when you're forty something and dating. This whole "putting yourself out there again," thing is starting to feel a lot like the ol' Hokey Pokey. "You put your whole heart in, you put your whole heart out, you put your whole heart in, and you shake it all about?" That's really not a bad analogy. Let's call it the Love Hokey Pokey. Sometimes you gotta know when to stop. Sometimes you have to recognize when your heart has had enough shaking and simply stop participating, and sometimes, you just gotta throw that whole heart in there and let love turn you around. Maybe that *is* what it's all about. Maybe dating and love all come down to how well you can do the Hokey Pokey. Who knew?

So, the Hokey Pokey aside, what I want to know is how does a woman hold onto her "power" in a relationship, yet still approach love with an open heart? Can you put your whole self in and still maintain your unique identity and not be thrown off your rhythm by the different rhythm of your partner's drum? How can you fall in love, yet still maintain your center? After a betrayal, how do you learn to trust again, and how do you maintain an inner calm despite the vulnerability that approaching a new relationship inherently requires? The first few dates, it's easy to keep a safe distance. The part that gets tricky is several dates and several weeks in, when you both feel a connection, see potential, but still don't know one another all that well. At this point, when you have a discussion where you both commit to dating only one another, is where the challenge to maintain a solid grip on the centered life I have worked so hard to build over the past eighteen months. I'm at the point where I don't want to be alone. I want a partner, a companion.

The answer I know to be true is that you have to stay connected to your Source, to God first. In my head, I know that keeping God first in my heart is the only way to keep my inner balance, but in my heart, I am feeling so thrown off in this moment. Dating at over forty has its own particular challenges that dating at twenty-two did not have, and I'm discovering there is potential to fall victim to a myriad of possible new insecurities at this age. Now, I have to be concerned with not only if my interests, personality, and dreams line up with a potential partner, but does he fit within the family I already have with my children? Will the kids like him? Will he like my kids? Will they get along? In particular, the man I am in this budding relationship with is twelve years older, which I think is a great thing for me at this stage of life. However, his kids are already grown. On one of our first dates I asked him, "How do you feel about being with someone who still has children at home?" His response was, "I've thought about that, and I wouldn't be sitting here with you at dinner if I wasn't okay with it." I have a six-year-old, which means if we ended up together long term, he would be committing not only to me, but to being a part of my daughter's parenting for more than a decade. I know that's a lot to ask, and I worry that maybe he will change his mind the further our relationship progresses.

The other scenario of dating someone my age means that he will also have school-age children at home. To me, this seems even more complicated. Not only do you have to get along with each other, you have to hope that children will get along. In addition, you would be balancing two custody arrangements and likely endless after-school and weekend extracurricular activities. Either way, it's complicated.

As usual, I over analyze every possible dating scenario before it even happens before realizing I really need to lighten up. So what if I didn't plan on having to do this dating crap all over again? Maybe it could be fun, after all. I mean, there could be worse things than dating, like being stuck living with a man who completely ignores you and disappears sporadically for days or even weeks at a time. Been there. Done that.

Maybe, just maybe, I may even have a little bit of fun along the way. You just never know.

Here's what I do know: be so busy being you in a big way that you're not even worried about looking for Mr. Right. I think the magic happens when you're in the flow of your purpose and content with what is right in front of you. I have a feeling that is when God is most likely to work -- when you're not even looking. I tell myself this as I pull out my lap top to write and get in the zone or when I'm in the middle of a conversation with my kids, that I'm right exactly where I need to be in the moment and already have a very full and fulfilling life. It does get lonely, but I think it's better to be alone than to be with the wrong person. So, hang in there. Once you stop looking for love, that's usually when it finds you.

SO, I DATED A SOCIOPATH

No, really. I did. Unfortunately, I didn't figure it out until it was way too late. What do I mean by way too late? I mean it was too late. I had let my guard down after ten months of dating, and I had actually started to believe in love again.

The problem was, my new boyfriend, the first one since my husband dumped me for another woman, turned out to be even more jacked-up than my ex-husband, which I honestly did not think was possible. It is possible, it turns out. As bad as what my ex-husband did and was to me, I don't think he set out to intentionally deceive me. I don't think he was intentionally manipulative until the very end and certainly was honest in the beginning of our relationship. Basically, I realized my ex-husband at least loved me honestly in the beginning and probably the majority of our marriage until the last year. I have no doubt in my mind that when we fell in love with each other, we were truly, honestly, completely in love. At least I had that.

The difference in being in a relationship with a sociopath is you look back and realize nothing in the relationship was even real. *Nothing.* It was all a giant hoax of smoke and mirrors: an illusion. I was part of a game he was playing to see how many "plates" he could keep spinning at once. It was about power. It was about control. By the time I realized those little red flags I had been ignoring or he had so flawlessly explained away, I had already been conned out of the one thing I had worked so hard to get back again: trust.

The ability to be able to trust again was something I wasn't sure was possible after my husband's deception. Now, I had been deceived again. Was I really that big of a gullible, naive idiot? I was really starting to wonder. My sister, Stacey, insisted there was no way I could have known and that he was just that scary good of a liar. My parents insisted the same thing. They had been around him a lot. They were so excited and happy that I was happy again and that this man not only seemed to adore and spoil me but also appeared to adore, accept, and actually pitch in and help with my children as well. Everyone around me assured me that he had us *all* fooled. My Uncle Jonathon, a psychotherapist in practice for thirty years, called to see if I was okay and wanted to talk. I wasn't okay, and I definitely needed to talk. He assured me that I could still trust myself and my own judgment. He explained that people like that are so adept at lying that it would be difficult for anyone to catch on.

The only silver lining I found in the situation was that it helped me forgive my ex-husband in some weird way. It also drove home the point to me that this man cheating on me had absolutely *nothing to do with me*. A light bulb came on for me. I realized that not only did this situation have zero to do with me and one hundred percent to do with this guy's warped thinking, but I also realized with absolute clarity that my husband cheating on me had *nothing to do with me*, either. It wasn't a reflection on who I am as a person. I was enough. I had always been enough. It was all about these men and their own issues that made them do what they did. It had never been clearer to me than that afternoon sitting in my sister's house in Austin, that the choices these men made to be dishonest was a reflection on themselves, not on me.

It wasn't that I wasn't attractive enough, fun enough, smart enough, or a "good" enough person. In fact, when I looked up the other girlfriend, it was clear it wasn't about looks at all. It was about power and control. There was one thing I didn't have that the other woman did, which was money. To me, that was the most disgusting admission from this man when I confronted him in the end.

The conversation went something like this: (Note: So as to not murder your eyes with a plethora of exclamation marks at the end of every single complete thought I wrote, just imagine me saying *everything* with "strong emotion" and an elevated, pissed-off tone of voice.)

Me: Why did you do this? Why did you lie to me? What did she have that I didn't?

Sir Liesalot: Nothing! I don't know why I did it. Honestly, I don't even like her that much as a person.

Me: You don't even *like* her? That's the stupidest thing I've ever heard. Is that supposed to make me feel better? You cheated on me with a whole other girlfriend you didn't even *like*? Well, you must like *something* about her if you were cheating on me with her. So, tell me what it was!

Sir Liesalot: She bought me drinks, okay? She drank a lot, and she bought me drinks, too. I wanted to drink, and she didn't question me or how much I drank. It was like having a drinking buddy.

Me: A drinking buddy … that you were also having sex with? Okay… What else?

Sir Liesalot: Honestly?

Me: No. Lie to me some more, please.

Sir Liesalot: The money.

Me: The *money?*

Sir Liesalot: Yes, the money. She had money, okay? She paid. She bought *me* dinner. She bought me things. It was nice to have someone pay for things for once instead of me always paying!

Me: (steam coming out of my literally poor ears) Are you *serious* right now? New flash, asshole: I'm a freaking junior high school teacher! If you wanted to date someone with money, why on earth would you date a *teacher?* Of course I'm not going to pay for dinner when you're the one inviting me out all the time! I never once asked to be taken to a nice restaurant, or a concert or anywhere, for that matter. So, let me make sure I get this straight. You cheated on me with someone you don't even like because she paid for dinner, bought you things, and you got drunk together a lot? All of this is according to you, so she's probably actually a really good person in reality. So based on what you've said, you basically you want an alcoholic, sugar mama, drinking buddy for a girlfriend? Awesome. End Scene!

Single people, here's a word of warning. There are some seriously messed-up psychos out there who are so good at playing the dating game you won't even know what has hit you until it is too late. The result? Disillusionment, distrust, and a suspicion that there may not be any good, quality, compatible men out there for the taking anymore. Ladies and gentlemen, it's a jungle out there. No, let me rephrase that. It's *worse* than a jungle out there, like *way* worse. At least in a jungle, you basically know what to expect if you're trying to stay alive. I mean, I would expect the obvious dangers in a jungle: snakes, spiders, poisonous dart frogs, jaguars, bullet ants. It's Jurassic Park. It's a jungle of terror on steroids.

Men and women are out of control. I include women because I've spoken to male friends who tell me there are women out there too who are just looking for sex and not a relationship. I've also talked to men my age who are single who think they are dating a woman exclusively and then, as I did, discover she had several men in her "rotation." Come on, people. At this age, we really don't have time to waste on you and your mind games. Like I told my ex: Just be honest! Obviously, if this happened to me and to other people I know, why don't all the people who just want "hook-ups" or to date a lot of different people just get together so you're not screwing with the rest of us? Seriously. My ex-boyfriend begged me to give him another chance.

He kept saying, "Is there anything I can do to fix this? Is there anything I can do to make it up to you?" My answer was an emphatic, "No!" Not unless he had a time machine to go back and erase his douche-baggery is there anything that could ever fix being betrayed, lied to, and manipulated. I told him there was only one thing he could do for me at this point, which was to simply stop. Stop lying to people. Stop telling someone they are the "only one you want," when the reality is, they are only one out of four or five that you want. Stop being gross. Stop womanizing. Just stop.

Here's a little story for you, a flashback. The story of how I met Sir Liesalot. The story of how one moment can take your life in the completely wrong direction.

It's December of 2016. It was my birthday, my 41st birthday, and I was coming to grips with the fact that my husband was indeed divorcing me and about to shack up with another woman in the house we had lived in together for the past six years. I was working on re-building the meager scraps of my self-esteem, and after my birthday dinner, my friend, Barbie, suggested we go dancing at a local honky-tonk. I didn't have anything else to do, and I do love to dance, so off we went.

This place we went to I can only describe as about as redneck as you can get. We arrived around 9:00 pm, way too early apparently for the "younger crowd." There we were, one married woman who just wanted to break in her new boots, one engaged woman, who was just along for the ride, and me, who just wanted to dance. So, we danced. We danced with Joe. Old Joe must have been in his mid-70's, but he could cut a rug. Then there was the hefty older cowboy gentleman with suspenders, a gray handle-bar mustache, and a cowboy hat who danced with all three of us. It was wild, I tell you. It was during this geriatric dance-a-thon that I decided to take a break from all the excitement and make a visit to the ladies' room. On my way out, I happened to pass by a very cute man. He had dark hair, a blue plaid shirt, Levi's, and an overall clean-cut look about him. He just looked like my type. I could tell he was my type because he didn't look like he fit in there at all. Before I could stop myself, I blurted out in rapid fire succession, "You're cute. Are you single? Can you dance?"

I know, worst pickup lines ever, but I really did just want to dance with someone at least younger than 70. He said yes, and he was a great dancer. He came back to the table where we were sitting after we danced, and my girlfriends started to grill him. It also turned out he had gone to Texas A&M University and was a fellow Aggie, like me. I could tell that by his Aggie ring, of course. We can spot each other from a mile away with those things. He said he had just moved to town because his dad was sick, and he was helping him out. He said he had retired from the Marine Corps and now worked for the federal government. As soon as the words, "Marine Corps" fell from his lips, my girlfriends' eyes almost popped out of their heads. I think my friend Tiffany actually shook her head, chuckled, and exclaimed, "Nope! Leave now!" I rationalized the Marine Corps issue by telling myself he was an officer, so surely, he wouldn't behave like my ex-husband. I was right. He behaved *worse* than my ex-husband.

My other friend Barbie tried her best to re-direct my attention back to our girls' birthday night out and away from my temporary boy-crazy state of the moment. If only I had listened to my friends. Maybe I was blinded by his stellar dancing skills, his intelligence, his confidence, and later by the fact that he pursued me. It had been awhile since anyone showed that much interest in me. He always had the next date planned with a concert, dinner, or some type of entertainment. He was well-traveled, well-educated with multiple degrees, well-spoken, and all around really did have his stuff together professionally. He also had a story about his ex. She was "crazy." Sound familiar? It turned out he probably drove her crazy because he is a big, fat lying womanizer.

What's the point of this story? I have a few.

Number one: Listen to your friends. They may be smarter than you think they are and know you better than you know yourself.

Number two: Don't meet men in redneck bar/dance halls. If you do, give it time before you decide to trust them.

Number three: Some Aggies *do* lie and cheat, contrary to our Aggie code of conduct. Not everyone is a rule follower.

Number four: Hindsight is 20/20. So, don't spend too much time looking back, just enough to know better the next time. I'd like to think that the next time I come across this type of person, my radar will go crazy warning me to run the other direction. I'll be asking for signs, signals, red flags, flashing lights, any warning signal at all. My radar is up. I know some ladies who have some unbiased radars who can scan the next prospect. So, instead of looking for a man to dance with, find yourself some friends with well-honed, impeccable, internal bullshit scanners who can help you discern the bad apples from the good ones! *That* is a worthwhile relationship.

DEAR UNIVERSE

I see what you did there... I see you, you sneaky, sneaky Universe. You have quite the sense of ironic humor. I have half a mind to be mad at you, as I sit here staring into my skinny peppermint mocha wondering what the hell just happened, but I know better. As much as things have been screwed up lately, I know you have my best interests in mind, and in spite of it all, I believe you are loving. I believe you're "for me," you know, in my corner, so to speak. I'd like to imagine you're cheering me on, at least in between the moments where you're cringing and squinting as you look away from the train wreck you knew was coming from a mile away while I was busy ignoring you and making stupid decisions on my own. I know who did this. I see her looking right back at me in the mirror every single day. I'm trying to forgive that lady.

I also know better than to blow off the fact that of all places at all times I would just coincidentally show up to spend some time writing at my local coffee shop at the exact same time as my painfully recent ex- boyfriend. You know the one I'm talking about dear Universe --the one who lead me to falsely believe we were in an exclusive, monogamous, heading somewhere long-term relationship while he was carrying on with multiple other women he was meeting on Tinder. That one.

If there is one thing I have learned about you, Universe, it's that there simply are no coincidences. This could only be an appointment made by You. There simply is no other explanation. So, now what I'm working on figuring out is what is my "take away" supposed to be from this encounter? Did I need some closure? Did he need some closure? Were you simply trying to give me some new writing material? Frankly, I don't really care what he needs, but I think you must be impartial. Maybe, you're teaching him a lesson, or maybe you're teaching both of us a lesson.

After two back-to-back betrayals by men, I'm starting to wonder if perhaps I was a real douche bag in a former life. Then the circumstances of the past eighteen months would make complete sense. Maybe I was a philandering playboy breaking hearts, taking names, and flying through women faster than Hans Solo in his Millennium Falcon escaping Darth Vader. I must have been a piece of work. So, if that was the case, do you think we can call it even now? Can we give Karma a call and yell "Uncle!?" Please, please, say yes. I'm just not sure how much more of this I can take.

Not only did you orchestrate my coming face-to-face with Sir Lies a Lot as I stepped onto the sidewalk to head into the coffee shop, you also managed to time it to occur approximately three minutes before my ex-husband, Sir Drinks a Lot and only lied a lot at the end, showed up as well. At least that was somewhat planned. I had to hand off some clothes our daughter needed while she spends the holiday at his house, and I happened to be pulling into the driveway of the Starbucks as he was exiting the freeway from wherever he was coming from before. It was another convention of the exes. Why does this keep happening? Maybe your purpose was to force me to ask myself, "Why?" I have a lot of "Whys?"

Dear Universe, what I sit here wondering now, post impromptu ex-meeting, is why I attracted two addicts, back-to-back? I know I'm an empath. That's why I felt compelled to get a Master's degree in counseling psychology. I know there is something in me that is meant to be a healer in some way. Is this why you had to break me down? No, I think I did that to myself. Maybe you're doing the best to straighten me out, get me back on the path, point me in the right direction. I truly appreciate that. If nothing, I have learned humility from all of this failure. I am learning forgiveness as well. I think I'm also learning an important lesson about control -- that there is no such thing as having everything under control, especially when it comes to love.

Control is an illusion, and as much as I have tried to control things and people around me, the truth is, I'm spinning my wheels in futility until I learn to let go. Did I just answer my own question, Universe? Are you trying to teach me to not hold on too tightly to people or things, but to allow them to come and go without fighting the currents of change and time?

So much has changed. As a matter of fact, I read about change just this morning. It was by your buddy, Wayne Dyer. He said the only constant thing in life is that things change. Well, he said it, but he got the idea from another book, the Tao. I know of another book that talks about there being a time for everything, Ecclesiastes, the third chapter, to be exact. It says there is a time for everything under heaven. It says there is a time to be born and a time to die, a time to plant and a time to uproot. Clearly, this is a season of time in my life of dying and uprooting. Relationships have ended, and my life as I knew it has been completely uprooted. Dear Universe, I think maybe I see what you did there after all. Wayne said something else about change that I read just this morning. I even underlined it in the book. He said that endings are really beginnings and instead of getting stuck in despair and depression over the endings, if we can see them as beginnings, we can find peace and purpose. That's really what I'm looking for after all, not Mr. Right, not Mr. Make Me Happy, but Peace and Purpose.

Dear Universe, I surrender.

Yours Truly,
Just a girl trying to figure this all out

HAVE POWER, WILL TRAVEL

Travel brings power and love back to your life.

—Rumi

What does travel have to do with divorce? I was trying to formulate my thoughts on the transformative effects of travel when I came across the above quote by Rumi, and it brought everything into focus for me. For me, a huge part of divorce recovery was learning to stand in my own power again. We hear phrases like, "Don't give away your power," or "Take your power back!" But what does that look like, and how does one go about owning your own power? Are we to beat our chests and shake our fists into the air atop a high cliff? No.

Taking your power back doesn't happen with one dramatic declaration but with a thousand small moments of decision.

I'm writing this from a seaside restaurant in Cape Cod, Maine, and after navigating my way around Boston solo last night, let me tell you, this trip has already reminded me I can stand in my own power. The fact that I'm from south Texas and have spent the last two days jumping into the crazy, whirling dervish of these northeastern "roundabouts," a traffic phenomenon as alien to a Texan as a winter blizzard, has helped me prove to myself that I really can make it on my own. It may sound simple, but when you've spent seventeen years in the passenger seat on every out-of-town trip, there's something both slightly terrifying and liberating about being the one in the driver's seat.

Aside from the inherent confidence builder of managing travel logistics comes the reminder that life really does still exist in a world outside of the comfort of the married life and partnership you once had. When my marriage ended, places we had been and things we had done together just brought up painful memories. Travel is an opportunity to create new memories. Traveling to new places and meeting new people is memory building.

Mark Twain wrote, "Nothing so liberalizes a man and expands the kindly instincts that nature put in him as travel and contact with many kinds of people." I agree, Mr. Twain. There is something liberating about discovering new places and meeting new people. There is something magical that happens to our awareness when we travel. We remember that there is a whole other world outside of the small one we have created for ourselves in our day-to-day lives.

When we travel, every day is full of new discoveries.

Today, it's raining here in Sandwich, MA, and I'm all by myself. Being alone gives me incredible freedom of choice. What a gift! I sat in my rental car this morning, opened my Google maps, and stared at the blank, gray search box patiently waiting for me to type in the destination of my choice. That's right, I said, my choice. In these moments, I realize that I need to enjoy every moment of being forty-something and single. I am alone with my thoughts, and the quiet and stillness make it easy to listen to my inner voice. To me, one of the challenges of relationships is holding your own inner compass, your own true north, in a life entwined with another person. One day, I hope I'll join that delicate dance again, but for now, I'm in the lead. So I see this time and this freedom today, not as a burden, but as a blessing.

Today, on this rainy Cape Cod Monday, I decide it's a great day to find a little local cafe and write. Beth's Bakery & Cafe is just a mile away, according to Google maps, so I fill that gray search line, turn on my windshield wipers, and take a right onto 6A. Beth's turned out to be a great decision. I just finished eating the absolute most delicious homemade cranberry scone I've ever tasted with a side of whipped cream and berry jam. I've written about eight hundred words in the past hour and a half while enjoying a perfectly made cappuccino with the background noise of the locals bantering jovially.

Soon, I'll be navigating the last roundabout of my trip before turning in my rental car and joining the masses in the lines of luggage and security in the bustling craziness of the Boston Logan airport. For now, however, I'll enjoy my last two hours of discovery and freedom before I return back to my daily life. It's a beautiful life I'm returning to, and travel is also a reminder that there really is no place like home and no people like the three little (six years), medium (thirteen years), and now tall (sixteen years) people I can't wait to get home to and hug.

As a matter of fact, my cell phone just lit up with a green text box from my six-year-old.

"Mommy, I love you to the moon and back. We made chilly!" This is what it's all about. Going home with a new appreciation of the people I love and who love me back and looking forward to driving back down a little Texas dirt road that dead ends at a house full of love and a bowl of hot, Texas "chilly."

SIGNS, SIGNS, EVERYWHERE SIGNS

The Universe will give you signs and winks if you ask for them. Ask for a sign and pay attention to what you receive.

—Gabby Bernstein

My dad used to tell me and my sister Stacey, "You'd argue with a stop sign." So, maybe I *am* a little stubborn, but I'd like to think I've outgrown arguing with signs of any sort, especially the "signs" that seem to come from the universe. Have you ever watched Steve Martin's movie, *The Jerk*? There's a scene where he's sitting in his office asking God to tell him what to do, to give him a sign. Sure enough, all kinds of signs start presenting themselves right around him, but he is completely oblivious to all of them! At one point, he says something like, "Please give me a sign! Just *any* sign!" as the picture on the wall directly behind his head is madly spinning around in circles.

Have you ever been that person? On the one hand asking God to give you a sign while on the other hand remaining completely oblivious to the flashing neon light blazing, "Hello?! Hello?!" right in front of your face? I certainly have. I've joked that God sometimes has to hit me over the head with a metaphorical hammer to get me to pay attention. Since my divorce, I have made a concerted effort to not operate on that level of oblivion any longer. My divorce taught me to pay attention. It's taught me to slow down and pay attention to not only what is going on around me but within me as well. It's taught me the value in stillness. It's taught me that I am only one mental shift of awareness away from peace. My divorce led me to the beautiful awareness that even when I feel completely and utterly alone, I'm not. God is, incredibly, miraculously, unbelievably close. It's taught me to seek hard after God and pay attention to what the Holy Spirit is speaking to my heart. I'm learning to listen, and I'm learning to follow.

With so much noise in the world, getting still and listening has been the best thing I have found in helping me recover from a toxic relationship and a painful discard and divorce. Disconnecting from my ex-husband and reconnecting to Spirit has been my main mission since September of 2016. Part of this mission was learning to pay attention to the signs around me. As usual, because I'm a words girl, a book came across my path that taught me in a pretty amazing way that it's okay to ask God for signs because well, He's God, and that's really not hard for Him! For me, the book *E Squared* by Pam Grout came across my path at a time where I needed a lot of reassurance that God was out there, and was hearing all of my desperate, middle-of-the-night prayers to heal my broken heart. So, at the risk of appearing weird, here are a few of my stories about the signs I asked for, and the signs I inevitably got. They did strengthen my faith, and they showed me that God has a sense of humor.

I hadn't really thought too much about signs until last year when I picked up Pam Grout's book off my dad's side table in the living room. My dad is historically good at picking out interesting books, so I grabbed a warm blanket, wrapped it around my shoulders, and sat down on the brown-leather couch that early fall morning and started to read. It was one of those books you don't want to put down, especially if you're forty years old, in the middle of a divorce, and your ex-husband has already taken up with a new girlfriend while you're still trying to figure out how he fell out of love with you without you even knowing it. In times like those, you'll at least give a book a glimpse if it seems like it may give you some kind of encouragement. If nothing else, it took my mind of how sad I was feeling.

As I started to read the first chapter, I knew I was going to be temporarily stealing this book from my dad until I finished it. First of all, this Pam lady is funny, and she tells her personal stories, which I like. Second of all, she has you do experiments. Who doesn't like to do experiments? Best of all, the experiments worked in pretty amazing ways.

I can't really explain it, you'll just have to try it for yourself. What I can explain is how it got me thinking about the impact our focus has on our lives. An example she gives is when you buy a new car and all of a sudden it seems like everywhere you look, you see your car! It's not that all of a sudden everyone went out and bought Ford Explorers. They've been there all along. The change is in your awareness. Now that you're driving one, you notice them where before you didn't. They were there, you just weren't aware.

Pam Grout refers to an "invisible energy force or field of infinite possibilities." Part of the description of the book says, "Rather than take it on faith, you are invited to conduct nine 48-hour experiments to prove there really is a positive, loving, totally hip force in the universe." Well, I already believed that, so I figured why not give these experiments a try? My life felt like it had gone to hell in a hand basket, so what did I have to lose? Instead of focusing on how sad I felt, I decided that if what you "focus on expands," as she was writing, I really didn't want to feel any more depressed than I did already sitting around crying over a very bad ending to a marriage. So, I started writing down specific requests with a time limit, and the miracles started happening. It was a lesson in awareness, focus and faith.

The first sign I asked for was a pink feather. I know that's weird. I was trying to pick something unmistakable. Like I said, hammer-to-head with me. So I imagined floating down to the ground, a bright, hot-pink feather. I wrote it down, and I gave the universe a time limit. The only problem was, I was at my parents' ranch in the middle of nowhere. I started thinking how absurd it was to ask for a pink feather to float out of the sky in the middle of a cattle ranch in central Texas where all you can see for miles and miles are cows, trees, grass, and dirt. I figured this experiment was doomed from the beginning. So, I got my piece of paper back out and decided to also ask for a purple butterfly as a sign. I don't know what my deal was with the colors, I guess I wanted it to be specific. So, I wrote it down, folded my paper up and hid it in my purse in case anyone might see it and wonder why I was asking the universe for a pink feather and a purple butterfly. I was questioning my own sanity at this point. I didn't want to give anyone else any ideas!

My parents were going to a fundraiser in the tiny "downtown" of Thornton, Texas and invited us to go along. So the kids and I jumped in the truck with them to head down to the little fire station in town. We went through the serving line scooping up pinto beans, a slice of white sandwich bread, and the most delicious smelling Texas barbecue you could imagine. We sat down at a folding table and started to eat and visit. As I looked across the table, I saw an older lady stand up to get in line. She reminded me of my Mamaw Ruth, with her short, perfectly coiffed, curled hair, brightly painted finger nails and lipstick and her colorful blouse. It was the blouse that really got my attention because guess what was all over it? Butterflies. Purple butterflies. I froze and for a moment wondered if it were just a coincidence. I hadn't told anyone about the experiment, so I quietly sat there grinning like a freak. It had been less than two hours since I had written that note to the universe, and there was the purple butterfly, lots of purple butterflies.

Then, the next morning as we were packing up to leave Thornton, my daughter said, "Mom! There's something in the grass!"

"What is it?" I yelled from inside. We were in the country, so I figured it was an animal of some sort and headed outside.

"It's a balloon!" she said.

Sure enough, there was a pink balloon in the middle of the yard ... a bright pink balloon had floated down out of the sky in the middle of nowhere and landed right in front of the house. My heart started racing. So, maybe a bright pink feather floating down was a tall order, but a bright pink balloon was close enough for me. I knew it was further confirmation that the Universe shows up when we pay attention, and that it definitely has a sense of humor.

After the butterfly and the balloon, it was on. I found an earring that had been lost for six months. That may not sound like much except it had been lost in a dirt parking lot. I was carrying the matching one around in the console of my car where I looked at it every day. A few weeks after the first experiments, I was putting my daughter in the car and looked down at the ground next to my car where I was standing. Right between my feet was the long-lost earring. I froze for an instant before letting out an incredulous, "No. Freaking. Way." I bent down to pick it up. The bright turquoise color had faded to a light green, but it was the lost earring. Amazingly, even though it had been in the dirt and pea gravel of a parking lot for months, not one of the small stones in it was broken.

It was all in one piece. I picked it up, and I've kept it visible in my room as a reminder to pay attention.

My favorite sign story, though, happened fairly recently. I had started dating this seemingly very nice man. This was after I discovered my first boyfriend post- divorce was a complete liar and player, managing a line-up of women like only a professional baseball manager could do with such ease. So, I was definitely not wanting to make another mistake. About six weeks into the relationship, I decided I needed a sign. It was a long-distance relationship, and I wasn't sure I was ready to go down that road. It had been a long time since I had asked for a specific sign, but I really was having trouble reading this man, and I needed some help. So, once again, I got out a sheet of paper one night before I went to bed and wrote out a request for a sign. I said a prayer, telling God how confused and scared I was to fall for someone again who might not be a good person. The last one was so good at hiding his true self, I was beginning to doubt my intuition. I really didn't want a repeat. I wrote out a prayer to God and ended it with a request.

"Dear God, I feel so confused as to what to do and I need your guidance and help. I trust you. You're the only thing I'm sure of and the only One I trust. Please give me a very visible "yes" or "no" sign. A thumbs up or thumbs down. A stop or go sign. A red light or a green light. Make it a concrete sign. Make it black and white -- no gray. Please make it so obvious even I cannot possibly miss it! I'll be looking for it in the next 24 hours. Thank you."

All the next day I looked for the sign, but it was such a busy day at work and with after-school activities with my kids, I thought I had been too distracted to be aware of it. I looked at the clock. It was 9:00 p.m., just a few minutes away from the 24 hours since I wrote asking for my sign. I was exhausted from the day, and I figured I would keep my eyes open tomorrow. I grabbed a shirt and yoga pants out of my laundry hamper of unfolded clean clothes, threw them on, and got into bed. I picked my Bible up off my bedside table and opened it to the Psalms to pray. As I took a deep breath and relaxed in the quiet stillness of my bedroom, it was suddenly as if someone flipped a light switch on my awareness. I had been so tired, I hadn't paid any attention to what I was wearing. I looked down at my shirt, and right there in the middle of my neon-pink shirt were the bold, black capital letters, "NOPE." Not only did it have the word, "NOPE" in the middle, "NOPE" was written up and down both long sleeves of the shirt! I got goose bumps all over and was struck with the sudden, silent knowing that this was most definitely the sign. I couldn't help but laugh out loud and tell God, "Well, I got it! I'm going to take that as a big, fat, NOPE!" It couldn't have gotten much more obvious than the fact I was literally wearing the "NO" in neon and bold, black letters all over my shirt. See, God can get messages across to even the densest of us when we ask, trust, and stay aware, and God definitely has a sense of humor. I mean, I asked for the old "hammer-over-the-head" sign, and the shirt got the point across!

D SQUARED

The past is over and cannot be changed. This is the only moment I can experience.

—Louise Hay

Are you familiar with American author Nathaniel Hawthorne's 1850 historical romance novel, *The Scarlet Letter*? If you weren't forced to read it as part of your high school English class, or if you aren't a literature junkie, I'm going to guess that's a big, fat, "No." Basically, the setting is in the 1640's in Puritan Boston, Massachusetts. The main character, Hester Prynne, has a daughter, Pearl, out of wedlock. Hester refuses to name the father. She is publicly shamed and further punished by being forced to wear an embroidered scarlet "A," for "adulteress," on her dress for the rest of her life. You'll have to read the rest to find out who the "baby daddy is:" no spoilers here. Hester and her daughter are looked upon as outcasts, shunned and isolated from the rest of the villagers. She makes her scant living and provides for her daughter with her beautiful embroidery. She is quiet, dignified, and spends much of her time helping the poor and the sick, but despite her good works, she must daily wear a physical reminder of her shame. I always loved the story, so when I started thinking about the feeling of shame I was experiencing in my divorce, Hester and her embroidered scarlet A kept coming to mind.

When I first imagined the cover for this book, I imagined a big, Scarlet D dominating the page or a big scarlet D with an exponent of 2 above it because divorced felt like a label I would never be able to shake. I felt ashamed and embarrassed to admit that I was divorced, much less divorced *twice*. I realize that "Divorced" is a label, like so many labels we are accustomed to slapping onto ourselves and others. I realize that the label of "Divorced" is not who I am. It has helped to shape me into the person I am today, but it is not *who I am*. My hope is that you, too, will come to see yourself as so much more than a label that defines your relationship status.

Dr. Wayne Dyer in his book, *10 Secrets for Success and Inner Peace*, calls this "transcending labels." He also urges the reader to, "find a way to transform your personal history." For me, writing has been a part of finding my way. Reading has also been a part of finding my way. In the quiet morning hours where I've made the choice to sit with my Bible and listen for God's still, small voice, is where I've given God permission to both mend and change my heart. When I've simply sat in my turquoise tulip chair in my backyard, wrapped in a fleece blanket, with a cup of coffee and my Bible or an inspirational book, these moments over time have added up to transformation. It's in the smallest moments of letting go that I've found myself again. I have built a habit of making time to be still and listen. In the chaos of change and upheaval that divorce brings, these moments of quiet reflection and meditation have been critical to helping me find and keep myself balanced and at peace. If you haven't already made this a habit, there is no better time than now to create a space and a time for intentional connection to Spirit.

It is possible to transform the pain and disappointment of your past. It is possible to acknowledge the pain and suffering you experienced, thank it for what it has taught you, and wave it goodbye. With that final wave, it is your choice to turn around and take one step forward and continue to move in a new direction, the direction of what is waiting right in front of you. New life is there with your eyes fixed on what is ahead. New life is also there right where you are standing, in the present moment. I learned that if I was going to be able to even move forward at all, I had to learn to accept the reality of the present. Somehow in accepting it, the twisting, thorny vines of the past wrapped around my feet were uprooted, and I was able to move ahead. There are new paths for you to discover or create. There is love on the road ahead, and there is peace.

I didn't find the peace and the love until I lost what I thought was my life, my husband, home, and a family as I knew it to be. In my most desperate hours, I knew where I needed to turn, and so I turned my eyes upward to the heavens. I knew that in my despair, there was One who was faithful. I knew that if I looked for God in the midst of the pain, I would find Him there. The Bible says that God so loved the world that he gave his only son to die for us so that we wouldn't perish but have everlasting life. I still believe that. What I don't believe is that it is my job to judge anyone else for what they do or don't believe. I also think that people find God in as many different and unique ways as He has created us. I don't believe there is a formula that one denomination or religion can claim as the only way to find God. I only know how I find Him, and I don't know anything else or claim to. This is what I know: I found God in the stillness of the night when my heart burned so hot with grief I felt as if I would die if I didn't find relief. I know that when I determined I would turn to the Psalms and read them back to God in the middle of the night, kneeling and weeping on a bathroom rug, the God of the universe comforted my heart. I read and prayed until the tears finally stopped and I could sleep again.

I know that every time I sang praise songs in church, lights turned down, tears streaming down my face, that my tears were silent prayers, and the tears of pain were always transformed into tears of gratitude flowing out of a thankful heart. I know that as I sat in church, holding back tears, hope welled up inside my heart that God was still a God who heals and redeems the broken. I knew I was broken, and I knew I could not fix myself. I asked God to heal my heart, and a funny thing happened. Every time I prayed and sought answers, they were there, and God sent people into my path to help.

My hope now is that I will be an answer to someone else's prayer for help in the middle of the grief of divorce. I hope that God will see me fit enough to use me as never before. After all, I think that's why we're here -- to love each other the way God loves us -- fiercely, fully, and fearlessly, even if we choose to reject it. The beauty of the loss of my marriage is that it led me more deeply into experiencing love than I ever have before. If you allow the grief to swallow you up, you will miss so much. Allow the loss to lead you back to or at least closer to the heart of a loving God who accepts us just as we are, right now.

In this moment, I can say without hesitation or doubt that I would not trade the disappointment and broken dreams set into motion on June 28, 2016 for where I am spiritually and emotionally today, February 18, 2018. Twenty months and ten days after the bottom fell out of my marriage, I am a different person. I learned that losing the love of your life doesn't actually kill you, even though it feels like your heart will explode. I learned that not only can I live without a man, I can be truly happy, contented, full of joy, and at peace without one. I discovered new gifts I didn't know I had and spent time developing them because my focus wasn't on pleasing someone else or worrying about trying to be someone else's conscience. I learned that I can control only myself and that I am not responsible for someone else's bad decisions, only my own decisions.

Without the betrayal, loss, and divorce, I wouldn't be who I am today, and guess what? I like who I am today way better than who I was twenty months ago. Twenty months ago, my father stood in my kitchen and told me that one day I would look back and realize that my husband leaving me for another woman was the best thing that happened to me since I married him. It made me angry at the time. *How can you say that? How can this be the best thing that's ever happened to me?* I thought. It turns out that my dad is a pretty smart man. He was right. It was the best thing that could have happened to me for so many reasons.

How can my divorce be the best thing that could have happened in that marriage? Easy. My husband didn't love me, and it had nothing to do with me. What I thought was love wasn't love at all. When you love someone, you come home to them. When you love someone, you take care of them when they need you. When you love someone, you listen to them without judgment. When you love someone, you don't abandon them for your buddies. When you love someone, you don't flirt with other women in front of your wife or behind her back. When you love someone, you stop doing the things they have told you hurts them. When you love someone, it looks like I Corinthians Chapter 13, not Jason in Friday the 13th. When you love someone, you stay. When you love someone, you show up. When you love someone, you fight for them even when it's hard and you want to give up. So really, what did I even lose?

Twenty months and ten days later I no longer see what I "lost." I see what I gained. I found myself again, and the beaten-down version of the woman I had become -- neglected, unloved, unappreciated, and invisible -- was magically transformed into a completely new person. I have new dreams I didn't have before. I have close, fulfilling relationships with my family and friends that I didn't have before because of the chaos surrounding my marriage. I gained the ability to let go of the false sense of control I thought I had and realize, I am not in control of anything but my thoughts and my own actions. I gained the wisdom to stop judging others and myself as well. Most importantly, I have a relationship with God unlike I have ever had before because as soon as I turned my heart back on Him, he was right there. I learned that He is always right there and that He is on my side even though I am so very flawed. God has met me in the dark places, knows every ugly place in my heart, and loves me anyway. If I gained nothing else from the grief of divorce, where I am on my spiritual journey was worth it.

HEARTBREAK AND TIME

Breaking Up is Hard to Do.

—Neil Sedaka/Howard Greenfield

Yesterday I was doing my weekly Wednesday morning bus duty in the seventh-grade gym. I enjoy Wednesday morning duty, despite the fact that I feel a little more rushed on those days, because I have the opportunity to "welcome our students to school," as our principal calls us to do every morning at 6:50 a.m. Yes, we run on junior-high school time. The time when only dairy farmers and secondary-school teachers are showing up to work.

Anyway, it's a reminder to me that these awkward adolescents, these middle schoolers, are indeed still tender at heart despite their best efforts at bravado. So yesterday morning, one of my favorite students walked into the gym, and I greeted him good morning. A few minutes later his seventh-grade girlfriend, Maria, walked in and stopped to talk to me at the door.

"Ms. Fife can I talk to you?"

"Sure, what's up?"

"I'm going to break up with Robert today, and I don't know how to tell him. What should I say?"

"Well, why do you want to break up with him? Do you like someone else?"

"No, but it's going to be summer soon, and we're never going to see each other. I think it's better if I break up with him now during the school year so he has his friends here to support him."

I glanced across the gym at Robert. He was smiling and laughing with his friends, clueless about what was about to hit him. I knew Robert by this time of year as a sweet kid, kind, tender-hearted, and good-natured. He was always polite, had a good sense of humor, and I knew that when he talked about this little thirteen-year-old girl who was about to dump him, his face lit up. Robert had a lot of things going on in his life that made him sad. I knew because he had written about them, and he and a couple of the other students in seventh period had started opening up a little bit by the end of the year. That's one of the things I love about teaching writing. It leads to conversation about topics that go deeper than pure facts and information. Writing is full of themes, lessons, and stories that can teach us about life.

I was painfully aware that Robert was about to experience firsthand knowledge for probably the first time in his young life about the reality of heartbreak. Robert was about to be dumped, and no matter how old you are, getting dumped is a little bit of a gut check. Everyone remembers their first heartbreak, even if it was "puppy love," or just a seventh-grade crush. Why? Because when you're "in love," or think you are, for a moment you feel invincible. Love can make you feel euphoric. It's the best thing in the world when it's good, but when it goes bad, it's the worst.

As I stood at the gym door watching this seventh-grade mini drama play out, I wished for a moment I could shield Robert from what I knew was coming. I knew in a matter of moments his happiness was going to come crashing down, even if it was only a seventh-grade level crash. The thought crossed my mind to suggest to Maria that she wait, or reconsider, but I knew it would be wrong to interfere. I watched as Maria walked over to the side of the gym where Robert was standing with his friends. I watched him smile as he saw her approach, and I watched as his smile faded while she spoke to him. It was quick. She clearly cut right to the point, and there stood Robert, face red, with tears already welling up in his sweet, brown eyes. He covered his face with his hands and turned toward the gym wall, attempting to hide his tears. A few seconds later two of his female friends who were also in my class tried to comfort him. One of them caught my eye as I watched them, and she pantomimed a tear rolling down her face as she gave Robert a big hug and rubbed his back.

Our counselor was kind enough to allow him and his friends to go sit in her office while she finished morning duty. As I walked past the counseling office on the way to first period, I popped my head in to check on him. He was slumped in the chair but not crying anymore.

"Hey Robert, how are you?"

"Not so good."

"I know. I'm really sorry,"

The tears started to surface again.

"Yesterday I was really upset about family stuff, and now today?"

"I know. You've had a rough few days. I remember yesterday wasn't such a great day for you, either."

In that moment, I tried to think of what I would want my older self to say to my younger self if I were in seventh grade and had just been dumped by my first boyfriend. I wanted to make it better, so I tried my best to give him the same advice I had been telling myself the past two years since my divorce.

"Robert, I know you're really sad right now. I know it hurts, but remember that what you are feeling is temporary. It's not always going to feel this way. I promise. Trust me. Life can be really hard sometimes. There are ups and downs. So when you're down, remember that it won't last. Just give it a little time, and you will feel better about this situation with Maria. I promise you will."

As I walked away down the hallway, bustling with the sounds of teenage chatter, laughter, lockers slamming, and the occasional squeaky sneaker, I tried to remember what it felt like to get your heart broken as a thirteen-year-old. It was a little fuzzy.

What I did know all about though, was exactly what it felt like to get your heart broken at forty. That I am very familiar with, but heart break at any age is never pleasant. As I thought about how terrible Robert was feeling, I thought about how much we as parents wish we could shield our own children from the heartache the world will inevitably bring their way. We can't stop them from getting their hearts broken any more than we can stop the sun from rising, but maybe we can be there to help them understand the fact that the young are simply too young to realize. It's not the end of the world, even when it *feels* like it's the end of the world. My hope is that maybe, just maybe, something I said this past Wednesday to seventh-grader Robert, he'll remember when he's sixteen, or eighteen or even forty-year-old Robert. Then again, maybe some things you can only learn the hard way. Maybe some of us, usually the stubborn kind, have to learn by falling flat on our smiling, love-struck faces. Either way, whether we listen and retain or learn by our failures, the lessons that love and heartbreak bring us are universal. At least when it comes to having your heart broken, you know without a doubt that you are not alone. You are in the company of millions who have found themselves fall from the heights of euphoria romantic love brings to the depths of despair that is the inherent risk.

All I know is that I didn't want Robert to hurt, and I wanted to find the words, any words, that would make him feel better. Just like I hoped my words would help ease the sting of being dumped, I hope that the words you've read here have somehow helped in even the smallest way.

WILL I EVER BE ABLE
TO LOVE AGAIN?

Have enough courage to trust love one more time and always one more time.

—Maya Angelou

You may be wondering if it will ever be possible to fall in love again. In the direct aftermath of divorce, I know I have wondered if it will be possible for me. The smart thing to do, I thought, would be to guard my heart forever and never allow myself to be vulnerable. This seemed like sensible, self-preservation. I doubted that I would ever be able to really trust someone again. Besides, I kept telling myself, "I have a great life! I'm happy where I'm at. I feel like my kids are happy and thriving. I love my job, and I have a nice routine." With everything being as good as it was though, I would have been lying to say I didn't want someone special in my life. How do you love again when you know what a risk it is?

I'm almost two years out from things falling apart, and I find myself for the first time starting to fall in love. I don't know how it happened. It just did. It happened when I wasn't looking and when I least expected it to. It happened in a moment of time when I was so happy and content it felt like my life couldn't get any better. It's beautiful, and it's terrifying. It's beautiful because now I know it's possible. It *is* possible, and I really doubted that! This feeling is unlike anything I've felt in a very long time, if ever. The circumstances surrounding my meeting this man could not have been coincidence. It feels like a divine intervention. I wasn't looking, and neither was he, but we came into each other's paths unexpectedly. It felt like an almost instant connection, not love at first sight, but we just connected as if it were effortless. While this feeling of falling in love is not new, it's different now that I'm older and have experienced the disappointment that falling for someone can bring. I'm old enough to know that a magical beginning may not mean a happy ending. I hope that it is, but at least now I know that if this ends, I am going to still be whole, complete, and perfect -- man or no man. I'm not looking for someone to "complete me." I'm looking for someone I can enjoy life with in peace and happiness. I want a companion, best friend, and lover. I want a relationship that's built on trust and honesty. I want someone with a loyal and kind heart, a sense of humor, and who is overall just crazy about me. I want emotional intimacy with someone who knows and wants an emotional and spiritual connection. Mostly, I want someone who looks at me in such a way that I can see the love they have for me in their eyes without them having to say a word. When we're young, we can be so naive. I was, anyway. I looked at the world through different lenses: lenses of blind trust and fearlessness. After my marriage ended badly and the sting of betrayal began to set in, I knew I had a choice to make. Do I choose disillusionment, distrust, and cynicism concerning all things dealing with the emotion of love? Do I build an impenetrable wall around my heart and soul that no one will ever be able to get through again?

How lonely that would be. How sad to let the fear of being hurt again keep me isolated, surrounded only by a collection of cats, muumuus, Netflix, and pinot noir. No, I would not build a moat around the cold, dark castle of my broken heart and never let the drawbridge down for anyone to enter. It is safe inside a place like that, but it's not living. It's survival, and I decided I want to live.

I know enough to know, however, that I did not want to repeat any patterns or have to make a go at learning life lessons I just hadn't gotten yet. I know that when we have unresolved pain, we attract someone from that energy. I truly believe that whatever energy level we're vibrating at and putting out into the universe will come back to us. We attract a vibrational match with the energy we send out. Whatever is in the subconscious that has not been brought into our awareness will attract a relationship to try and work it out yet again until we have learned the life lesson. The last thing

I wanted was to lower the heavy, wooden drawbridge before all was secure inside my heart. I was determined to make sure I learned all that I could from the failure of my marriage. I believe that the essence of who we really are is spiritual more than anything. So, doesn't it make sense that just like our physical bodies grow and change, our spirits are here for the purpose of growing and changing as well? Much of whether or not we grow spiritually depends on our choices.

In my quest to find someone to help me "get" the spiritual life lessons I was supposed to get from my failed relationships, God was faithful to bring me into the orbit of some very wise people. God moves through people. God loves us so much that he orchestrates what may seem at first glance to be "coincidences" but what I believe are divine appointments. It's amazing the small miracles that happen when we are paying attention, connected to, and listening to the still, small voice of God. God is as close as our heartbeat and the air in our lungs. God is as close and as real as the rays of sunshine we can feel warming our skin.

As I mentioned earlier, it was no accident that I ended up at The Crystal Bay Hotel in St. Petersburg, Florida in January of 2017, just a few weeks before my divorce was finalized. I had to get it through my head that I did not need a man to be complete, whole, and perfect. After Dr. Tong helped bring this awareness and I returned home, it was as if the next year presented the perfect classroom to help me get the lessons. When I left Crystal Bay Hotel, I knew I would be returning one day. It was a little over a year later that another surprise turn of events catapulted me into another round of healing.

I discovered that until I was able to truly forgive my ex, there was a huge roadblock to progressing further down a path to healing and wholeness. Forgiving seemed to be the choice that cleared the way for the other lessons. Strangely enough, it was when I discovered the first boyfriend I got serious with after my divorce was cheating on me that flipped some internal switch that opened the door to forgiving my ex-husband for cheating on me. Maybe it was the fact that this boyfriend was so calculated and manipulative. While it didn't make it okay, I knew that my ex-husband probably didn't plan to have an affair but started something that snow-balled into something more. Whatever it was, I was able to finally forgive. Forgiveness allowed me to let go of control. I realized there are things we simply cannot control, like another person, for example. I overcame the cheating boyfriend so much easier because I hadn't made him my God. I knew he was just a man, and that I didn't need him to make me happy. I came to understand that I am never alone or separate from God, from the Source that created us. What I knew my whole life or had been told my whole life, is that Jesus loved me and that God had a plan for my life; this moved from a nice idea to an unshakable, undeniable knowing of the truth. So, when I traveled back to St. Pete in March of 2018, I was in a much different mind frame from the mess I was fourteen months prior.

I traveled back to meet again with Dr. Tong because while I had been happily moving forward with life, when I found out my ex was getting married and wanted my daughter to come for a week in the northwest to be a part of it, it hit me. I was in shock that he was actually choosing to get married, and the feelings of rejection that still had some hidden roots in my heart began to sprout into self-doubt, sadness, and anger. I prayed. I cried. I cursed the grief that I thought was gone. Then I talked to my mom, and I called my sister Stacey and my best friend, Jenny. My sister was like, "Well, he is marrying the woman he cheated on you with and ended your marriage over, so duh! Of course you're going to be upset! Just remember how much better off you are without him. Now he's her problem. Not yours!"

Jenny always has a way of reminding me as well that I really should be focusing on the positive: the fact that I am free.

Me (sobbing): Jenny, he's marrying her.

Jenny: What?

Me: He is getting *married!*

Jenny: No freaking *way* …

Me: Yes. *Way.*

Jenny: When?

Me: May 5… Happy Cinco de Mayo. This is definitely going to require a margarita.

Jenny: Cody, it's not going to work. He hasn't changed. You know that.

Me: I *don't* know that though. But what if he *has* changed? What if he finally got himself together after all the years of me begging him to act like a husband? What if he changed, and now *she* gets the benefit of all the crap *I* put up with because he finally got the lesson from messing everything up with *me*? It isn't fair! What the hell? He's getting *married*?

Jenny: He *hasn't* changed. He was a complete jerk to you, remember? He's always going to be that way. He treated you like crap. He was awful to you. So, who cares if he's getting married? Better her than you!

Me: I know! So, what is *wrong* with me? Why do I even *care*? I thought I was fine. I was totally *fine*! I mean, I really, *really* thought I was *fine*. But this doesn't feel fine. This feels *bad* … Really, *really* bad.

Jenny: It's rejection. This is bringing up all the old feelings of rejection like you felt when you first found out.

Me: Why do I feel so *sad* all over again? This is ridiculous. I shouldn't even care.

Jenny: Cody, you feel *rejected*.

Me (light bulb coming on): You're right. It *is* rejection. But why do I still feel rejected? It's been a year. Shouldn't I be *over it*? Is there a freaking expiration date on this whole grief thing or what?

Jenny: That's not really very long, and *hello*? He cheated on you with this woman, and now he's *marrying her*. What the hell? It's *normal* that you feel this way.

Me: So, I'm *not* crazy to feel this way?

Jenny: Definitely *not* crazy.

I hung up the phone after talking with Jenny and had a little talk with Jesus. I told him that I *trusted Him*. I asked Him to please help me heal completely down to the last remaining speck of hurt left in my spirit and mind. I told God I was lonely, and that I hoped one day He would bring someone wonderful as a companion and lover. I kept hoping I would meet someone who blew me away, but I worried I would be in danger of "settling."

I knew I needed to head back to St. Pete to meet with Dr. Tong. As much as I was trying my best to stay positive and focused, I was having a hard time shaking the whole impending marriage of my ex. It felt a little like a ticking time bomb. I knew the closer the countdown got to zero, the more grief I would inevitably feel. Naturally, it made me remember our marriage, our engagement, and the broken promises he made to me. I had to fake a smile and nod when my six-year-old showed me a picture of the shoes her new soon-to-be step "mom" was ordering her to wear at the glorious Cinco de Mayo nuptials. I had to acquiesce to my ex asking to pull her out of school for an entire week during the end of the school year to attend this baloney.

So, I went back to meet with Dr. Tong, and he helped me put things into perspective. He did a guided meditation to anchor the belief that I am never alone but always connected to God. He told me my new mantra for the year was, "Who cares? So what?" "So, your ex-husband is getting married? Who cares? So, what? You got the lesson, and you get to move forward and be free from it. Would you still want to be married to him?"

"If he had been able to change and be a good husband, then yes," I said.

"But he isn't going to change. You are better off. Now you can move forward. You will find a complementary soul, and you will have a happy, fulfilling, very special relationship."

"You're right," I said. "Who cares? So what?" I repeated back to him, and for the first time since I found out he was getting married, *I really didn't care!*

At the end of our session he said, "You have them all. You've gotten all the life lessons." I was pretty sure I had, but I was really happy to hear the confirmation from him. These lessons had not come easy. They were painful. He told me that God did have a special person for me, and he asked me if I remembered how to send the intention out to the universe to attract that special person who was a complementary soul. He reminded me of a few things.

#1 *You have to have a strong connection with God first* and be secure in that. Never again make another person your "god." By keeping God, you know, the *actual* God, at the top of the list, your world won't fall apart if your partner checks out for good.

#2 Set the *intention* to attract your complementary soul. Not someone exactly like you, but someone who has strengths you don't have and vice versa. Someone you could move through life with connected to on more than just a physical level but a spiritual and emotional level as well.

#3 *Stop looking.* He said that it would happen when I wasn't looking for it, unexpectedly. He said that typically the man would move faster than he normally would, for example; and would likely tell you he loved you fairly early on. He said he would love unconditionally, without judgment and would never leave because he would know that God brought me to him. He said that both of us would know almost instantly, that we would feel the connection. He said that I would be able to know it in his eyes. He said that I (the woman) would set the pace for the relationship. I took literal notes as he spoke, and I felt excited at the possibility of God bringing someone special into my life.

#4 Say *yes* to invitations and opportunities that come your way. You never know where you might meet this person. By saying yes to invites, you open the door to possibilities.

This is a very basic and incomplete summary of some of the things we discussed, but you get the general idea. So, I thanked Dr. Tong and headed back upstairs to my room. It was nearing dinner, and even though this was my second trip to St. Pete, I still hadn't even seen the beach. I was determined to see the sunset, but I had no clue where to go. So, I Googled "best beach restaurant near St. Pete," and a restaurant called Caddy's on the Beach popped up. Several other ones came up as well, but I decided to give Caddy's a shot. The sun was about to go down, so I jumped in an Uber and headed across the bridge to Treasure Island and St. Pete Beach.

I wasn't sure if I would make the sunset, but as the driver pulled up to the restaurant, I saw the most beautiful view. Caddy's is right on the beach with picnic tables in the sand. You couldn't get any closer if you were looking to eat at the beach. It was cool and windy, and the sun was a beautiful ball of bright, golden orange. It had probably been at least two years since I had stepped foot near an ocean, so just being there felt like heaven. I breathed in the smell of the ocean, the sound of the waves, the feel of the soft, white sand as I slipped my shoes off, and looked out at the sunset with the most grateful and full heart. In this moment, I was happy. In this moment, I had peace. Fourteen months after first stepping foot in St. Pete, Florida with a broken and heavy heart, I was back, but everything was different. I was different. I was better: better than I had ever been. This time my heart was whole. This time I didn't feel lost. I had found myself, and more importantly, I had found God again.

This magical place, St. Pete, that only divine guidance could have brought me to the year before at the lowest point in my life, was a huge part of that journey. I know that God works in wonderful and magical ways because he loves us so much, too much to leave us broken in a dark valley. He had led me beside the still waters. He had restored my soul. Surely goodness and mercy were following me all the days of my life, and more than anything, getting my heart broken showed me the beauty of "dwelling" in the presence of the Lord.

There's a song I love called *Oceans*, by Hillsong United, and I would sing it out in the car on the way to work last year while I was in the darkest place of grief. The chorus sings, "So I will call upon Your name and keep my eyes above the waves when oceans rise, my soul will rest in Your embrace for I am Yours and You are mine." Standing next to the ocean that evening, I remembered and gave thanks for how faithful God had been to me through the stormy waters of the past two years, and I gave thanks for the knowing I had in my heart that God was always here, just a breath away. I knew that no matter what happened in my romantic love life, I already had more love than I could ever hope for or imagine.

Looking out at the waves that night as the sun set, it didn't matter that I was divorced … twice. It didn't matter that I was in many ways starting over at forty-something. I wasn't divorced and forty. I was just *me*, and I *liked this person* who really didn't even exist two years ago. Sometimes you have to learn how to love *yourself* again. I knew that the past didn't matter; that what mattered was what I decided to do with the rest of my life and all the moments there were to come.

While I don't know what will happen in the future, I do know that whatever happens will be okay. I do know that I will be okay regardless of whether I am in a relationship or not. I am blessed already with so much love, love for my children and my family and friends, and love for my Heavenly Father, who I know has and will never leave me. I am excited about what the future holds, and I am ready to leave the past where it belongs: in the past.

Where I am now is standing on the shore of a sea of infinite possibilities. So, I will let the waves come. Guess what? I can't stop them. I will choose to be right where I am. Even though there was a lot of noise and crashing, I listened closely. I looked for peace and love and found it again in my relationship with God. I knew I would arrive at this place if I just held on long enough, trusted, and stayed aware of all the good flowing toward me and through me. I knew one day I would wake up and truly realize I am never alone.

My hope is that you will know this peace too, no matter what stage of divorce and grief you may be in. We are beautiful, and where we are now is not the end. Where we are now is standing on the shore of a sea of infinite possibilities. Let the waves come. Guess what? You can't stop them. Be where you are. Even though there's a lot of noise and tumult, if you listen closely it sounds like peace rolling towards you. Take heart. It's on its way to where you are.

TIME FOR A REMODEL

My house is currently under construction. Everything is covered in dust, there's plastic everywhere, a paper runway taped down over my floors, and electrical outlets dangling by wires hanging out of my newly taped, floated and painted sheetrock. My dishes are displaced, my toaster is nowhere to be found, and my refrigerator is sitting in the middle of my kitchen plugged into an extension cord.

Everything is in disarray, and it doesn't feel good. It feels great. As discombobulating and uncomfortable as it is to have everything in my house out of order, I'm excited about it all coming together in the end.

This house was my grandparents and was built in 1971. While I am thankful for it, it was ugly. I'm certain that at the time it was built, avocado green, harvest gold and orange seemed like a winning combination. I'm also sure the dark, wood paneling covering the entire living room, kitchen and part of the bathrooms was also very much in style then, and so were orange polyester bell bottoms… Some trends just need to die. It was time to make some changes. It was time to tear some shit up and replace it.

My boyfriend, Kevin, (yes- an actual *boyfriend!)* happens to have quite the eye for design. He has a knack for looking at broken down buildings, and spaces in general, and seeing them not for the condition they are currently in, but for what they *could be or can be.* That takes both creativity and vision, both of which are just two reasons I love the man. He is in the business of transformation, in the non-metaphorical sense. He buys crappy, crack house-esque apartments and makes them lovely and livable again.

While I had a vague idea of what I wanted to see this house transformed into, he showed me a picture a few months ago from a photo on Houzz. Actually, first he asked me, "What would you think about painting your fireplace brick black?"

"*Black*? Hmmm. Well I had planned on painting it *white*, but what's your idea?"

He showed me the picture on his phone, and that became the vision for what the goal is for this house. Having a vision for the future- such an important starting point for any new beginning. So, slowly we began making changes.

After much deliberation at the Home Depot paint department, we settled on a charcoal paint color and went to town painting the fireplace. Kevin took me to a home design store downtown, and after hiking up four flights of stairs to the discount section on the top floor, we happened to come across two fantastic chandeliers. We took down the old, dark brown and brass fans. Up went the chandeliers, and voila! Magic. With just two small changes, the entire room was transformed.

Sometimes the big changes can seem overwhelming when you look at all that has to be fixed or replaced, but if you take it one small change at a time, it becomes manageable.

I look back at where my life was two and a half years ago, and I see how much I've healed and how far I've come. Making repairs just takes time and patience. Healing a broken heart doesn't happen overnight. Just like a remodel can be a real pain in the ass at times and all you want is for it to be finished, the same can be said for grief. There is no "easy" button. There is no fast-forward arrow. You simply have to take it one small change at a time.

Also, just like in home repair and remodeling, you may find that the job is simply too overwhelming to do it alone. Maybe you need to find someone who is an expert and can speed the process along. I found that as I got my spiritual "house" in order, God (Source) never failed to bring people into my life to help me along the path. There was Dr. Mark Tong and his retreat center in St. Pete, Florida, whose guidance, wisdom and faith helped remind me how big and how loving God is. He helped me begin to let go of what was not meant for me and believe that God's perfect plan for my life was not a fantasy but a real thing. Just like Kevin showed me a picture of what *could be*, so did Dr. Tong.

Dr. Tong told me after my second visit to see him a year ago, that he thought I was ready to set an intention for a "complimentary soul mate. " By complimentary he meant someone who was strong where I was weak and someone who was weak where I was strong. He explained that the bigger purpose of the relationship would be growth, and we would grow together. So, we did just that. We set the intention. I grabbed hold of a vision for my life that included love and a partner I could grow and move through life with. He told me to practice saying "yes" to invites as you just never know when you will cross paths with someone who would end up being the life companion I long for.

Three months later, an acquaintance who my friend, Barbie, and I had met out dancing over Christmas texted that he was in town visiting his parents. He asked if we would be up to go dancing again. The last time I had gone was six months prior, and I do love to dance. So, even though I was tired, I said yes. Barbie and I arrived around 10:00 and headed in to meet our friend. A few dances in, a man approached and asked me to dance. What a surprise when he turned out to be an amazing dancer. I mean, a *phenomenal* dancer. Barbie, our friend, and I all danced, but after my second dance with this man, I just kept hoping he would stick around. He did. He hung around us for the rest of the evening, but I couldn't tell if he was interested in me. I'm a little slow sometimes.

As the dance hall was about to close, I still couldn't tell if he was interested, but the fact was he wasn't sure if the friend I was with was my date. He disappeared for a minute, and then he walked over to me as I sat in a bar stool next to the dance floor.

"Well, I think I'm about to head home, and I know I'll probably never see you again, " he said.

"Well, that would be sad," I blurted out.

"What?" he asked.

"If I never see you again," I said. "That would be sad.

"Let me ask you something. Well, first of all, are you married?"

"Ha! *Hell* no," I laughed.

"Ok, well you'd be surprised." he said. "If I were to ask you on a date, would you go with me?"

"Yes. Definitely," I said.

He asked me to come over to the bar, grabbed a napkin, a pen from the bar tender, and wrote my name and number down on a napkin, then wrote his name and number down on another napkin for me. As he wrote, he had a few follow up questions to the "Are you married question."

"So, are you a vegan?" he asked.

"I live on a cattle ranch...so, that would be a no!" *Weird question*, I thought.

"Do you like to travel?" he asked.

"Well, duh... who doesn't!" I said.

"You'd be surprised," he said.

He handed me the napkin. His name, Kevin, and his number were written on it.

I handed him my napkin, name and number included.

The next morning, my phone dinged the familiar "You've got text" ding.

It was him.

"So, I know I'm breaking the three-day rule for contacting you, but at my age, I really don't have that much time left."

Okay. He's a great dancer. He's cute, and he's funny!

One first date and eight months later, I'm forever grateful he didn't wait three days to text me. At the end of July, Kevin booked us a trip to Puerto Vallarta and a magical stay at a breath takingly beautiful boutique hotel called Verana. It was during our week together in Mexico that I began to fall in love with Kevin Baker, and it was on this trip that he told me for the first time, as a swarm of yellow butterflies flew over our heads, that he was going to marry me.

He has told me that countless times over the past eight months, and if you want to know the truth, if he does ask me for real one day, I would probably, most likely say yes.

That is a miracle. I said that I would never, ever, never get married again. I know. Never say never.

While the prospect of getting married again may seem crazy to some people, it isn't crazy to me. Call me Elizabeth Taylor, but I haven't completely given up on the whole idea. You get three strikes before you're out in baseball, so I figure that's a fair rule of the game. If I strike out three times in the game of love, you can count me "out," but for now, you can count me "in."

Love has been a long time coming for me. While dating Kevin has been beyond anything I could have hoped or dreamed of, it hasn't been 100% full of unicorns and rainbows. Trusting has not been a picnic. Learning to trust has been no less than torturous at times. The after shocks of betrayal have left a mark, and I am constantly learning and maybe even more challenging -*unlearning*.

There are times that my knee jerk fight or flight has me wanting to sprint, full force, for the hills. I am grateful that in my moments of every cell in my body wanting to "take flight," I have found a man who keeps gently turning this tender and terrified heart back to him. He isn't perfect, but like he always tells me, he's perfect for me. I am also far from perfect, but together, we make each other better.

I cannot predict the future. I cannot change the past, and while I struggle at times to live in the present, I can only say that I'm doing my very best to move forward and to grow. I'm doing my best to not live life constantly looking over my shoulder or waiting for the other shoe to drop. Maybe, like writer Alan Cohen says, *there is no other shoe*.

The truth is, sometimes it feels much safer to not love anyone. If you don't allow yourself to be vulnerable, then no one can hurt you. If you put up impenetrable walls around your heart, you are guaranteed safety. One of the bravest acts is to choose to love again knowing full well you risk getting hurt. The way I have to look at taking the risk to love again is that I have no control over another person's choices, and if the person I love ever chooses to betray my trust, that had 100% to do with them and 0% to do with my worth. I do know that, and I learned it the hard way.

I have a feeling that this season of remodeling- this season of doing away with the old and replacing it with the new and improved was all a part of a grander plan. I also have a feeling that meeting Kevin was a part of that plan as well. Life lessons are best learned in the context of relationships, and I know that God uses people to help us learn and grow if we allow it. There are no coincidences, just divine appointments.

I look around at my house today, and I see how beautifully it's all coming together a little at a time, and I look inside of myself and see the same process unfolding. One day at a time, my heart has been healing. It was time for a remodel, and I think God knew who the perfect person was for the job.

Made in the
USA
Middletown, DE

77515599R00119